DR SCHWEITZER, O.M.

Dr Schweitzer in his room at Lambaréné
From "The Africa of Albert Schweitzer" (A. and C. Black), by
C. R. Joy and M. Arnold

Fr.

DR SCHWEITZER, O.M.

*The Story of his Life and Work,
for the New Generation*

BY

NINA LANGLEY

AUTHOR OF
"EXPLORATION IN THE ANTARCTIC"

GEORGE G. HARRAP & CO. LTD
LONDON TORONTO WELLINGTON SYDNEY

First published in Great Britain 1956
by George G. Harrap & Co. Ltd
182 High Holborn, London, W.C.1

Reprinted: 1956; 1957; 1958

*Composed in Imprint type and printed by
Western Printing Services Ltd, Bristol*

PREFACE

I WISH to express my gratitude to the authors and to Messrs A. and C. Black for permission to quote from *Albert Schweitzer*, by G. Seaver, *Music in the Life of Albert Schweitzer*, by C. Joy, and from Dr Schweitzer's own books *On the Edge of the Primeval Forest* and *More from the Primeval Forest*, and to Messrs Allen and Unwin Ltd, for the use of passages from Dr Schweitzer's *My Life and Thought* and *Memoirs of Childhood and Youth*.

Reference has also been made to *The Africa of Albert Schweitzer*, by C. Joy and M. Arnold, and to *Albert Schweitzer: An Introduction*, by J. Feschotte, both published by A. and C. Black, to the authors and publishers of which I feel myself indebted.

N.L.

CONTENTS

ILLUSTRATIONS

*Dr Schweitzer at the organ some time in the
nineteen-twenties*

An old-time pirogue. To-day the hospital dug-outs are manned by lepers who have been cured at the hospital

INTRODUCTION

ON the banks of the great river Ogowe, in French Equatorial Africa, stands a hospital. It is not a hospital of bricks and mortar such as would be found in an English town. It comprises about forty buildings, some small, some large, built on hundreds of piles driven into the ground. Its walls are of wood and corrugated iron and it has corrugated-iron roofs. The great river Ogowe flows past its foot, and on for 175 miles to join the ocean, and at its back is the African primeval forest, rising like a dark wall a hundred feet high and stretching far away into the interior.

There are bread-fruit trees round about the hospital buildings, and huge kapoks, and coffee-bushes, and orange, lemon, grapefruit, and other fruit-trees. Geese, hens, turkeys, ducks, sheep, and goats wander at will between the wards, monkeys swing from trees and roam the verandas. Parrots fly about, weaver-birds build their nests in the palm-trees, a pelican perches near, tame antelopes of diminutive size gambol about.

Besides these friendly pets, the great primeval forest is alive with fierce wild animals—panthers, gorillas, poisonous snakes, and all kinds of insects—and in the river are the crocodile and the hippopotamus, swordfish with a sword a yard long at the end of their jaws, and electric fish which can sting a man so that he loses the use of his limbs and is drowned.

This would seem a strange spot at which to build a hospital. One might wonder who would choose to come to a hospital in a place like that. The answer is that almost all the patients who come to this hospital are black patients—African Negroes, who often suffer from terrible complaints and diseases that we know nothing of.

It would need a brave man to plant a hospital in these dangerous surroundings for love of his brothers the black men, but a brave man did it. This is the story of him and how he did it.

EARLY DAYS

ALBERT SCHWEITZER was born in Kaysersberg, an Alsatian village, on January 14, 1875. When he was about six months old his parents moved to another village, Günsbach, where he was brought up with his brother and three sisters in a very happy family.

His father was the village pastor (as the clergyman of the Protestant Church was called), and his grandfather on his mother's side was also a very well-known pastor, Pastor Schillinger. Both his grandfathers and some of his great-uncles were fine organists, and so little Albert was born with the gifts of preaching and of music 'in his blood.'

From the age of three or four he used to be taken to the services at the village church at Günsbach, and he looked forward to this all the week. Sometimes his childish attention would wander up to the organ loft, where there was a mirror hung so that the organist could see the pastor's movements and know when it was time for him to play and when to stop. The organist's face was reflected in the mirror, and little Albert imagined that it was the devil, who had to flee quickly when the prayers or Bible reading began.

There was only one church in Günsbach, and, as was the case in other churches in Alsace, the Roman Catholic priest and the pastor would use it in turns for their services one after the other. There was no rivalry but only friendliness between them, and while each held the kind of service he thought right and proper they each respected the opinions of the other, which until we shall all be united in one way of thinking would seem a much better idea than that of trying to hold a service to please both and which really pleases neither.

The Protestant pastor thought chiefly of praying and preaching, while the Roman Catholic priest's principal service was the Holy Communion service, called the Mass. To little Albert Schweitzer it seemed a lovely idea that the same building should be used by both, and, though he belonged to the pastor's family and their services were mostly in the nave, he loved the far-reaching distances of the chancel, where the eye could wander and the spirit be lost in worship. And this led him when he grew to be a man to decide that it is a good thing for little children to be brought to church to worship God, even if they do not altogether understand the service.

There is another story which Dr Schweitzer has told about himself as a little boy. If you look at a picture of him as he is now you will notice how wiry his hair is and how it sticks up and will not lie flat on his head. When he was a child it was just the same. The maid who helped to look after the children used to brush it hard and plaster it down every morning with brilliantine, but after about an hour it had all jumped up again and there was no parting to be seen. She used to tell him that his hair was like his character, "Unruly within—unruly without," and this saying very much depressed the little boy.

Then one day he saw a painting by a famous artist of St John the Evangelist, and he noticed that the artist had painted St John with a mop of tousled hair like his own. This cheered him very much.

"Untidy hair didn't stop St John from being an apostle," he thought to himself. "So perhaps it is not true that your hair tells your character."

When the time came for him to go to school he was sent to the village school in Günsbach. But though he was the pastor's son, he intensely disliked to be considered 'a sprig of the gentry' and wished to be like the village boys in everything so that they would accept him as one of themselves. Because they wore fingerless mittens, he would not wear gloves, and, because they wore clogs to school and leather boots only on Sundays, he wanted to do the same.

One Sunday there was quite a scene before church. Albert's mother had made him a nice new overcoat from an old one of his father's, but he refused to wear it, because none of the village boys wore overcoats.

He was not a particularly clever boy at the village school, being rather too dreamy. However, he showed a gift for music, and at about the age of seven astonished the school-mistress one morning by playing a hymn on the harmonium, inventing harmonies in the bass as he went along, whereas she used to play only the tune with one finger.

Albert loved all animals, and when he went to bed and had said his usual evening prayers to his mother and she had kissed him good-night he used to say another little prayer which he had composed himself: "O heavenly Father, protect and bless all things that have breath; guard them from all evil and let them sleep in peace."

One of his playmates suggested to him one day that they should go shooting at the birds with some home-made catapults. Albert did not like to refuse for fear of being laughed at, but he purposely aimed crookedly so that his shot went wide of the bird. Suddenly the bells of the old church rang out. They seemed to him a joyful reminder of the commandment, "Thou shalt not kill." He turned and ran home, and after that he made a

B

resolution to be strong-minded enough to refuse to do
what he felt to be cruel.

We shall see later on how this idea remained with
him long after he grew to be a man.

In course of time Albert outgrew the village school,
and when he was about nine he began to attend a bigger
school called the Gymnasium at Mülhausen. He had a
great-aunt and -uncle living here who had no children
of their own, and they offered to let him live with them
during term-time so that he could go daily to school.
It was a two-mile walk each way, a walk thoroughly
enjoyed by the boy, who at first very much missed the
freedom of his home-life at Günsbach.

He made fair progress at this school without being in
any way outstanding. His great-uncle and -aunt brought
him up in a kind, though strict, fashion, for which in
after years he was very grateful. He still showed good
promise in music, though never very willing to practise.

"You never know what use your music may not be to
you later on," his great-aunt said one day, when she had
to drag him to the piano. Many years later he recalled
this saying, as we shall see.

When he was fourteen or fifteen he took piano lessons
with a famous organist, Eugen Münch, but they did not
at first get on very well together. Albert still liked to sit
down and improvise music, as he had improvised the
harmonies to the hymn-tunes in the village school at
Günsbach, rather than settle down to practise seriously
the music his master set him to do. Münch used to call
him his "thorn in the flesh." cause of constant trouble

One day, after the master had made an unusually
cutting remark to him, the boy decided to give him a
surprise. He took great pains all the week to practise the
piece he was set (one of Mendelssohn's *Songs without*

Words) and played it as he had never played before. He had his reward, for the master was pleased. He began to introduce the boy to the music of Beethoven, and then Bach, and as a final proof of confidence told him that after his confirmation, soon to take place, he would be allowed to practise on the great organ in St Stephen's Church with its three manuals and sixty-four stops.

A year later, at the age of sixteen, he had made such progress that Eugen Münch entrusted him with the organ accompaniment to Brahms' *Requiem*, which was being performed.

And so the years went on, and the time came for saying good-bye to the school and taking an affectionate farewell of his great-aunt and -uncle, who had for so many years occupied the place of mother and father to him.

We have seen how even as a little boy he loved animals and wanted to be friendly to all those he came in contact with. He was beginning to notice and be saddened by all the suffering he saw around him in the world. He was full of gratitude for his own happy childhood, to his father and mother for making it so, and to other friends as well.

Gradually it came over him in a vague way that, in exchange for all this happiness and for his good health, he ought to do something for those who are not so happy and who are ill or in pain. He remembered how our Lord had said that we must not use our lives for ourselves alone. It was not all clear to him yet, but we begin to see how the little boy who disliked cruelty to the birds, and who did not wish to have privileges not shared by his poorer schoolmates, and who liked a church where there was not jealousy but friendliness, was beginning to grow up into the man who in later years was to give his life to founding a hospital for Africans on the edge of the primeval forest in Africa.

However, many years were to pass before then. Albert was looking forward immensely to the years at the University which were to follow when he left school.

At the age of eighteen, with all the world before him, he entered the University of Strasburg.

CHAPTER TWO

THE GREAT DECISION

WHEN Albert Schweitzer entered the University of Strasburg in 1893 at the age of eighteen the two subjects he decided to study were theology and philosophy. His interest in theology was, of course, inherited from his father and from his maternal grandfather, Pastor Schillinger. He was already quite a good Greek and Latin scholar, and knew a little Hebrew. He found this last rather uninteresting, but it was required for the examination he would take in theology, and so he determined not to be beaten by the difficulty and eventually became quite a sound Hebrew scholar.

But what interested him most of all in his theological studies was the life of Jesus as told in the Synoptic Gospels, those of St Matthew, St Mark, and St Luke. When he had been at the University a year he had temporarily to give up his studies in order to do his compulsory military training. He went off for this, taking his Greek Testament with him, and when the year's training was over he went back to the University more and more interested in the study of the Gospels. He studied with increasing enthusiasm the life of our Lord, His words, His parables, His teaching, His character.

He began to consider his own great blessings—good health, loving parents, kind friends, happy work—and the thought kept returning to him again and again: "What have I done to deserve all this?" He remembered that Jesus had said: "Unto whomsoever much is given, of him shall be much required," and realized that we must not take our happiness as a right but must give something in exchange for it.

This thought began to join itself to that other thought he had had when he was a boy—sympathy with all the pain and sorrow he noticed in the world around him.

Gradually these two thoughts mingled together in his mind and from them grew the idea that it was the duty of all those who had been given happiness and spared pain to pay back, so to speak, something by helping to lessen the unhappiness and pain of others.

It was one bright morning in 1896 when he was at his home in Günsbach for the Whitsun holidays, with the sun shining and the birds twittering outside the window, that he came to a decision which was to alter the whole of his life. He was then twenty-one, and the decision he made was that he would give the next nine years of his life (until he was thirty) to the subjects he loved, theology, philosophy, and music, and after the age of thirty he would devote the rest of his life to some work for others less fortunate than himself. He did not know at all yet what work it would be to which he would give himself, and certainly he never thought at this time that it would take him as far from his native land as Africa.

At first he thought of doing something to help homeless and friendless children. He even went so far as to plan to perpetuate this good work by training the children he first should rescue to help other similarly-placed children. However, in the end this idea came to nothing.

Another thought he had was to help tramps and discharged prisoners. He and a friend did for a time do some of this kind of work, but Schweitzer came to the conclusion that to be really effective it would have to be properly organized.

But the important thing to him was to have made the decision. He knew that when the time came the matter would be made clear to him, and from the decision he never wavered. He kept it as a secret within himself, and then, when his holiday was over, returned to the University and threw himself again with zest into his studies.

Besides his work in theology and philosophy his other great interest was music. The little boy who had made up his own harmonies to the hymn-tunes at the village school, the schoolboy who had been such a "thorn in the flesh" to his earliest music-master, Eugen Münch, at Mülhausen until they learned to understand one another, and who had been so thrilled after his confirmation at being allowed to take lessons on the fine organ at St Stephen's, was now developing into a fine musician.

He has himself given the credit to his master for having "brought him on so well" that he considered him now ready to profit by a little tuition from the well-known Charles Widor, organist of St Sulpice's, Paris.

Schweitzer had an aunt and uncle living in Paris, and just before going to the University he had paid them a visit, during which he had presented himself before Widor asking for an audition at the organ.

"What will you play?" Widor asked.

"Bach, of course," was Schweitzer's answer.

Widor had been much impressed by the playing of this young Alsatian, and, though there was thirty years' difference between them in age, a lifelong friendship sprang up between them.

When the holiday in Paris was over and Schweitzer had begun his work at Strasburg University he took lessons from Ernest Münch, brother of his old Mülhausen teacher.

Ernest Münch used to get up Bach concerts, and Schweitzer would play the organ accompaniments during rehearsals. Eugen Münch would come over himself and play when the concert took place, but as time went on, and he was sometimes too busy to be present, Schweitzer used to be entrusted with the organ part at the concert itself as well as at the rehearsals.

The time went on, and four years after entering the University Schweitzer wrote his first thesis in theology. This thesis had to be a long substantial essay on some given subject, and the subject set this year was one connected with the Lord's Supper, a subject after Schweitzer's own heart. His thesis was successful and gained for him the "Goll" Scholarship. This was a travelling scholarship and enabled the winner to go where he wished, with the stipulation that he must within six years at longest take the degree of Licentiate in Theology at Strasburg, or forfeit the money given to him.

Schweitzer would have liked to take the whole six years for travelling in various countries, and to have spent part of the time at an English university, but he saw that one of his fellow-students was somewhat in need of money and so, very unselfishly, decided to spend less time in travel and take the Licentiate degree sooner than he needed so that the scholarship could then be awarded to his comrade.

With the scholarship he went first to Paris and there began to study hard at philosophy, for which subject he intended to write a thesis on the philosopher Kant.

In Paris, too, he naturally sought out his friend Widor, of St Sulpice's. Widor gave him organ lessons without asking any payment, and he also took piano lessons from two different teachers. He has told us that the two teachers were not quite in agreement between themselves.

They taught the piano each from a different view-point, but as long as Schweitzer remembered to play for each in the way that that one required the plan was successful.

Helped by conversations with and encouragement from Widor, Schweitzer, young as he was, began even then to make plans for a great book on Bach, to be written in French. The old Lutheran hymn-tunes were called chorales, and Bach had loved the chorales and written a number of Preludes for the organ based upon them. In these Chorale Preludes Bach had used a device of his own. He would take a small fragment of melody or harmony and use it continuously to express grief, or hope, or exultation, or joy, or some other feeling. Now, Widor was French and did not know the words of the old Lutheran Chorales, only their tunes. He one day confessed to young Schweitzer, his pupil, that some of these things in Bach's music puzzled him. They seemed to be rather 'bits and pieces' of tunes sometimes. Schweitzer was an Alsatian, and equally at home in French and German, and he knew all the old hymns by heart. He explained to his master that you could not really understand the music unless you knew the words, because the words explained the music. At once it became clear to the older man, and he was not ashamed to tell publicly the story of how his young pupil had helped him.

While Schweitzer was in Paris he was studying hard at his other university subject, philosophy, and he began to write another thesis, taking as his subject the philosopher Kant. When he returned to Strasburg he read his thesis before the Faculty of Letters at the University. It was approved of, and he was made a Doctor of Philosophy at the early age of twenty-four.

In December of the same year he was appointed as a preacher at the church of St Nicholas, Strasburg. He had to hold children's services, confirmation classes, and to teach and preach, all of which work he loved. The next year he took what was called the Licentiate in Theology and this enabled him to obtain a post as lecturer in the University. In 1903 he was made Principal of the Theological College of St Thomas attached to the University, a post which he had temporarily held two years earlier. As he still continued to preach and teach at St Nicholas's Church, his life must have been a busy one. He was also working in other directions during these years. His great book on Bach, written in French, was published in 1905 and achieved an immediate success.

In 1905 he and his friend Widor, in collaboration with five other musicians, founded the Paris Bach Society for the express purpose of giving concerts of Bach's works, especially the cantatas and the Passion music, as Ernest Münch had done at Strasburg. The stipulation was made that Schweitzer was always to be the organist at these concerts, and, as he was then living chiefly in Strasburg, it must have meant a good deal of travelling to and fro.

He was now, at the age of nearly thirty, famous in three different branches of learning—theology, philosophy, and music. It would have been natural for him to have built on these successes and gone on rising to greater and yet greater heights until he became a world-famous figure.

But he had not forgotten the decision he had made for himself that sunny Whitsuntide morning in his home at Günsbach nine years before. The wonderful thing about the resolution was not the making of it (for we know ourselves that to make a resolution is a very easy thing), but the keeping of it. All through these years of his continued successes he had kept it working in the back of his mind, and now the time was coming when he would have to put it to the test. The question was—where? He did not himself at all know, and if we had not already read the introductory chapter of this book and so had a glimpse behind the scenes we should never have guessed what form his service for others was to take. The most natural thing would have been to have gone on as he was doing at present, teaching and preaching to generation after generation of theological students about the Bible and the love of our Lord.

Or it would have seemed a reasonable thing to give one's life to giving concerts in every European capital and devoting the profits to charitable concerns.

But one day Schweitzer found on his table the magazine of the Paris Missionary Society, and in it he read an article setting forth the great need for doctors among the natives of French Equatorial Africa, especially to fight the terrible disease of sleeping-sickness.

His mind was made up at once. He would re-enter the Strasburg University as a student, train as a doctor, and go out to help the African natives in their need. He had been preaching to people for years about the love of Jesus, and now he wanted to go somewhere, where, instead of speaking of it, he could show it forth in deeds, as "love in action."

It was characteristic of Schweitzer that when once he had made a decision he never looked back. On October 13, 1905, he posted letters in a pillar-box in Paris to his parents and other friends, telling them what he had decided to do.

He was met with surprise and a storm of disapproval

on all sides. Why, if he wished to serve the natives of Africa, not go simply as a missionary, he was asked? He had already the gifts necessary for that calling, whereas he knew nothing of a doctor's work.

But he remained quite unmoved. "I wanted to be a doctor that I might be able to work without having to talk," he wrote in *My Life and Thought*,[1] and so, in the autumn of 1905, after having been a professor, he again became a student, this time in the Medical Faculty of the same university in which he had won his other honours.

The medical course would take at least six years, possibly seven, and he knew that it was going to be a great strain on him. His tastes all lay in other directions, in music, in preaching, in teaching, in writing, and he had inherited these gifts from his ancestors. None of them had ever been in the medical profession. But, with the same perseverance with which he had attacked Hebrew just because he did not like it very much, did he now attack his medical studies.

At the beginning of 1906 he gave up his post as Principal of the Theological College, but at first he still kept on with much of his other work, preaching at St Nicholas's Church, lecturing at the University, playing the organ at the Paris Bach Society's concerts in Paris or sometimes in Barcelona, Spain. He was also engaged in the writing of two or three books on different subjects. One of them was his big book on Bach, originally written in French, and now rewritten at greater length in German.

He did not in the least like his medical studies at first. Sometimes he would come out of a lecture very tired and dispirited. On these occasions he would go to the

[1] Published by Allen and Unwin (1954).

church where Ernest Münch was organist and have "an hour of Bach," which refreshed and calmed his spirit. But he never for a moment faltered in his resolve and went working solidly on, taking one examination after another, till at last the time came for the final one to be taken. This was in December 1911, and when he had passed it he could hardly believe that the long years of strain were over, and he was now a fully qualified doctor.

The following year he went to Paris to take a special course in colonial medicine to fit him for the place to which he meant to go. During his university years he had had a faithful friend and one who took an interest in all his doings in Helene Bresslau, daughter of the History lecturer at the University, and when his medical course was complete they were quietly married. She fully shared all his aspirations, and during this time had been training as a nurse so that she could go out to Africa and help her husband in his work.

With sadness in his heart he preached his last sermon at St Nicholas's from the text: "The peace of God which passeth all understanding keep your hearts and minds in Christ Jesus." [Philippians]. He then collected a fund of money which he judged would enable him to run a hospital in Africa for two years, since he did not intend to accept any pay for what he was going to do. St Nicholas's Church and other Alsatian churches collected money to give to the fund; the Paris Bach Society, whose organist he had been, devoted the proceeds of a whole concert to help him; and the rest he earned himself by giving concerts and by using much of the profits made from the German edition of his book on Bach. He used to say that it made him feel as if Bach himself, the old Cantor of St Thomas's School in Leipzig, had helped him to found a hospital for black people in Africa. His great-aunt's words—"You never know what use your music may not be to you later on"—also came back to him. He certainly had never imagined in those days that his music would help him in founding a hospital in the primeval forest.

When at last he had collected what he considered a sufficient sum to equip a hospital for two years he wrote to the Paris Missionary Society and offered himself formally to them as a doctor.

Now all was ready, and silently and without show Dr Schweitzer and his wife set off on their mission of healing. It was on Good Friday 1913 that they left Günsbach.

CHAPTER THREE

INTRODUCTION TO LAMBARÉNÉ

TWO days after leaving the little village of Günsbach where his childhood had been spent, Dr Schweitzer with his wife arrived in Paris. It was Easter Sunday, and they went to St Sulpice's Church and heard again the wonderful old organ played by Widor, with whom Schweitzer had maintained an unbroken friendship for twenty years. After the service they had to catch the train for Bordeaux, and then to take a boat for an hour and a half's sail down the river Gironde to Pauillac, where they would board the boat which was to take them to Africa. The boats bound for the Congo are specially built with very flat bottoms to enable them to travel farther up-river on reaching Africa, and so when at last they were in the open sea in the Bay of Biscay they had a severe tossing, with the trunks chasing one another from end to end of the cabins. It was a real storm, and it lasted for three days, until they drew near to Tenerife, where the boat anchored for a few hours while coaling operations took place.

Now that the weather was calmer the passengers, who during the storm had hardly been able to keep on their legs, were able to walk about and get to know each other a little better. Dr Schweitzer thought himself especially fortunate that there should be on board a military doctor who had already had twelve years' experience of the tropics and who spent about two hours each morning giving him what information he could about tropical diseases and tropical medicine.

From now onward, although the weather still seemed quite fresh and cool, every one was advised not to go about on deck without a sun-helmet. They were warned that it was quite possible to get sunstroke even on a cloudy day, and sometimes the sunrise or sunset was more dangerous than the full heat of the midday sun.

After a few days the boat drew into the harbour of Dakar, in Senegambia, and here they disembarked for the first time on African soil. Dr Schweitzer, with his love for animals, was distressed at the cruelty he saw here. He noticed two Negroes in charge of a heavily-laden cart which had stuck in the middle of the road. The Negroes, who evidently knew no better, were beating and shouting at their horse in order to make him move while they sat at ease on the cart, adding to its weight. The Doctor, stranger though he was, went up to them and insisted on their getting down and helping to push behind. He lent his own strength too, and, between the three of them, added to the horse's efforts, the cart was at last persuaded to move.

After this they had to rejoin their boat, which from now onward was almost always within sight of the familiar outline of the West African coast, the Pepper Coast, the Ivory Coast, the Gold Coast, the Slave Coast. Though the slave-trade no longer goes on, the name still persists.

On April 13, a Sunday, they reached Libreville. This, as its French name tells us, was originally a place set aside for freed slaves to live in. Eight hours later they reached Cape Lopez, the place at which the river Ogowe joins the sea. It was April 14, about three weeks since leaving Pauillac, and this was the last night they were to spend on board the ship which had brought them. The long journey up the river to Lambaréné would have to be made by river steamer and then by African canoe.

As they drew in to the harbour of Cape Lopez a feeling of apprehension seized the Doctor at the thought of all the luggage which would have to pass through the Customs. They had brought seventy cases with them, and their fellow passengers had warned them that they would probably be charged 10 per cent. duty on all of them. However, the Doctor explained matters to the official and showed him a list of all the things in each of the seventy cases, which were largely to be used for the hospital, with the result that they were treated kindly in the matter and went to bed with lighter hearts.

The next day they transferred to a small river-boat called the *Alembe*, in which they were to travel more than 150 miles up the river. There was no room for the seventy packing-cases; they had to be left behind and would follow in the next steamer a fortnight later. Only personal luggage could be taken now.

The journey up the river took a very long time. It started at 9 A.M. and went on hour after hour almost as in a dream. The black African pilot, who sat guiding the ship with the great wheel in his hand, knew his way well and took the steamer through the maze of side-channels, lakes, and waterways that make up the river without map or chart.

After some time a small Negro village was reached, and here several hundred logs of wood were taken on board. The Africans themselves did this work. One was in charge of counting the logs, and when ten logs had passed he called out to another who had a paper in his hand, "Put a one"; then when ten tens had passed he called out, "Put a cross." So the counting of the logs was done.

C

A little after sunset (6 P.M.) they reached a store, where as many as three thousand logs were counted out and taken on board. This took some time, and by now darkness began to fall, as it does very swiftly and suddenly near the Equator. However, the *Alembe* pursued her course up the river by moonlight, guided by her faithful pilot, who had been going up and down the river for sixteen years and knew it like the back of his hand.

At midnight they anchored in a quiet spot, and the passengers crept into their mosquito-nets (very necessary here) in the cabins or the dining-saloon for a short sleep.

By five o'clock next morning the *Alembe* was off again. They had gone about 130 miles by now, and before long they reached N'Gomo, the first of the Paris Missionary Society's mission stations. More logs were shipped here, necessitating a two hours' wait, then they were off again. The next place to be reached would be Lambaréné.

Five hours later the slopes of the hills of Lambaréné were seen in the distance, and half an hour later the village was reached. But the mission station was still an hour's journey farther on, in a side-stream where the *Alembe* would not go.

Suddenly in the distance is heard a sound of singing, and round a bend in the river comes an African dug-out canoe rowed by a crew of merry schoolboys. Behind them comes another, manned by bigger boys. They have come from the mission station to greet their new doctor. Some of the missionaries are with them, and the canoes have had a race to see which will reach the landing-stage first. The smaller boys have won, and so they have the privilege of taking the Doctor and his wife in their canoe, and the bigger boys will take the luggage.

The boys stand to row the boat, striking the water with long paddles and singing to keep themselves in time. It is a little frightening for the newcomers at first, for one slip might upset the whole canoe. A few miles farther on the canoe turns off into a side-stream of the river, and at last the bright light of the sun reflected on the windows of the mission station is seen.

Very soon the canoe comes to rest in a quiet little bay; the long journey, which has been very tiring, though full of interest, is over.

At the mission station some of the other missionaries and some of the black African Christians come out to greet the Doctor and his wife, and to shake hands in European fashion. Then the new arrivals are taken up to their little wooden bungalow on the middle one of the three hills.

It has four rooms and is built on piles, with a veranda running round. The view is entrancing—water, forest, and, in the distance, a line of blue hills.

Soon a bell sounds. It is for the little African children to assemble in their schoolroom for evening hymn and prayers. The Doctor and his wife begin to unpack in their new little house, but it is now sunset and the darkness falls. The journey by river-boat and canoe has taken two days.

The Doctor and his wife have supper with the missionaries, and outside the children sing a song composed especially for the occasion. The words have been written by one of the missionaries, and the melody is a Swiss folk-tune. It is a song of welcome.

Then the Doctor and his wife are escorted with the aid of lanterns back to their own little bungalow, and it is time to think of retiring to rest. But before they can settle down for the night there are large spiders to chase, much larger than the largest European ones, and flying cockroaches.

After a little all is quiet, and the Schweitzers compose themselves to sleep for the first night in their new surroundings.

CHAPTER FOUR

THE FOWLHOUSE HOSPITAL

BEFORE continuing the story of Dr Schweitzer's adventures in Africa, it will be of interest to read a little description and explanation of the country to which he and his wife had come to work.

The river Ogowe, on which stand Lambaréné and the other mission stations belonging to the Paris Missionary Society, is between 700 and 800 miles long, more than three times as long as the longest English river. In fact, to travel its entire length would be to travel a distance greater than the whole length of England and Scotland, from Land's End to John o' Groats.

The Ogowe runs parallel to a still longer and better-known river, the Congo. Explorers once thought that if you went right to the source of the river Ogowe it would be found that it joined the Congo, but it was proved that this was not the case.

The whole district now belongs to the French nation and is part of French Equatorial Africa.

The upper and middle reaches of the long river run between prairies and woods on either hand, but in the lower reaches, from N'Djole to Cape Lopez, where it joins the sea, there is nothing but water and virgin forest, water and virgin forest, for mile after mile after mile after mile on end. You can shut your eyes as the river-steamer carries you along and open them again an hour later and find yourself still in the same kind of surroundings, water and virgin forest, water and virgin forest. Pepper-trees grow here in abundance, and cinnamon, cocoa, and vanilla, coffee-bushes, and tall oil-palms.

Though this district belongs now to the French nation, it was not they who founded the first mission there. The Portuguese had started a mission station on the coast early in the sixteenth century, but the first Protestant missionaries were Americans, who came there about the year 1860.

But after some years the French Government proclaimed that the French language was to be used in all the schools of the district, and, as the Americans did not feel able to comply with this rule, they felt bound to resign their missionary work. It was then taken over by the Paris Missionary Society, to whom it still belongs. So from henceforth all the little black African children in the schools had to learn their lessons in French, and French was the language their fathers and mothers used when speaking to the missionaries. Dr Schweitzer himself was completely bilingual, speaking (as well as his native Alsatian dialect) both French and German with equal ease. In fact, he had already written and published books in both languages.

The Paris Missionary Society owned four mission stations on the Ogowe river. The one nearest to the river mouth, but 140 miles from it, was N'Gomo, and then there followed Lambaréné, Samkita, and Talagouga, each about thirty-five miles from the last. Opposite Talagouga was a place called N'Djole, where the Roman Catholics had a mission station, as well as one in Lambaréné and one at Samba, on a tributary. N'Djole is the farthest point to which the river-steamer can go; after that one has to travel on a small screw-steamer or by African dug-out canoe.

Lambaréné was the place at which Dr Schweitzer was

going to start his work as doctor, and he would be the only doctor (except the African witch-doctors) for 300 miles around.

The Lambaréné mission station had been built on three hills and occupied a narrow piece of land half a mile in length, but only about 120 yards broad. On the middle hill of the three was the little wooden bungalow, where the doctor and his wife would live. On one of the other hills stood the boys' school, the storehouse, and (on the slope down to the river) the bigger mission house, and on the other hill was the girls' school and the smaller mission house.

Twenty yards behind them (barely as far away as the length of a cricket pitch) lay the great primeval forest, a thick, impenetrable wall nearly a hundred feet in height, cutting off every little breath of air which might have helped to temper the intense heat (for it is but forty miles south of the Equator) and hiding within itself who could tell what of mystery and danger.

For the European the danger was chiefly that of the fierce wild animals which inhabited the forest, but to the imagination of the primitive African it was alive with evil spirits of which he lived in perpetual dread.

There used once upon a time to be eight different tribes of Africans living around these parts, but many of them had almost died out, largely owing to the slave-trade, which was practised until in the nineteenth century the French and English joined together to stop it. The two principal tribes now inhabiting the Ogowe lowlands are the Galoas, a peaceful tribe, and the Pahouins (or Fangs), a more savage folk from the interior with a cannibal background.

The Africans live in their own villages along the river banks or in clearings in the forest, in little huts made of

mud bricks, or of wood from the forest, and roofed with
leaves. They live very largely on bananas, of which each
family will have a plot, and about every three years a new
banana plot has to be laid out, because the old one has
exhausted the soil. A clearance has to be made in the
forest, often at some distance from the village, and this
entails much hard work, for great trees have to be felled
and then burnt, the ashes making manure for the new
plantation. This cutting down of trees is the responsibility of the husbands, but, once planted, the banana plot
has to be looked after and kept in order by the wives.

It was about the middle of April when the Schweitzers
arrived in Africa, and that is towards the end of the
rainy season. As Lambaréné is south of the Equator, the
seasons are the opposite from ours, but in any case they
do not quite correspond. The rainy season, which is the
summer, lasts from about October until the end of May,
except for three or four weeks round about Christmas
time, when there is usually a break in the rains and some
beautiful summer weather with the greatest heat of the
year. During the rainy season the temperature is anything from eighty-two degrees to eighty-six degrees
(Fahrenheit) in the shade, and the nights are not much
cooler than the days. The dry season, which is the winter,
lasts from about the end of May until October, but even
then the temperature does not fall much below seventy-
seven degrees. It is a very trying climate for Europeans
not brought up to it, and if they are to continue to do
good work it is usually necessary for them to take a holiday from time to time and come home for a few months
to our more temperate regions.

This, then, was the country and the people to whom
Dr Schweitzer had decided to devote the remainder of
his life. I cannot help thinking that his spirits must have

sunk a little that first evening as he went round chasing the spiders and flying cockroaches in his little bungalow bedroom. He did not know it then, but in later years Africa was to become like a second home to him.

At six o'clock the next morning the bell of the mission school rang out, and soon afterwards the children were heard singing their morning hymn. The Doctor and his wife got up to prepare for their first day's work among the native people of Africa. They only had with them a few bandages and medicines brought in their trunks, for the bulk of their luggage, the seventy cases, had been left behind at Cape Lopez till the next river-steamer should arrive in a fortnight. A notice was therefore given out that only the most serious cases of illness were to be brought to the Doctor for the first three weeks, so that he could settle in. However, not much attention was paid to this, for the Africans were so pleased at having a doctor among them again that they came to him at all hours of the day.

He had two great difficulties to contend with at the outset. In the first place, he could not speak the languages used by the Africans, and had to rely upon anyone who happened to be able to translate into their languages from French, the language used by the missionaries and by the Doctor. The second difficulty was almost greater: there was no hospital building at all in which he could examine his patients or treat them. The missionaries had promised that there should be an iron building put up, but they had not been able to have this done yet, because at that time all the African labourers available had gone to work with the timber-traders, who were able to pay them better wages than the missionaries could afford to.

On April 26, about ten days after the Doctor's arrival

in Africa, the seventy packing-cases unexpectedly arrived. The Doctor had had one anxiety, and that was about his piano. It seems strange to think of a piano out in Africa at the edge of the primeval forest; but when he had left Europe, the Paris Bach Society, which he and his friend Widor had helped to found, and whose organist he had been, had presented him with a beautiful piano made especially for the tropical climate. It was lined with zinc, and it had organ pedal-attachments— that is long wooden pedals beneath the feet as an organ has. Of course, the pedals would not make the sound of an organ, because there were no organ-pipes and no wind, but they would put down the notes of the piano to which they were attached, and, by doing this, enable the doctor to keep himself in practice against the day when he might, on holiday, be able to play again on a real organ.

The Doctor was very anxious about this precious piano when the seventy cases were being unloaded from the river-steamer and stowed on the canoes ready to be brought up to his bungalow. He did not see how it was possible to put a heavy piano on a frail canoe. However, a store was found which possessed a huge canoe made from the trunk of an enormous tree and capable of bearing three tons' weight. On this was placed the piano, and so it arrived safely at its destination. How all these heavy things were transported up the hill from the landing-stage to the bungalow it is almost impossible to imagine! But every one on the mission station, even the little black woolly-haired children, lent a hand. Two of the missionaries from the lower mission station at N'Gomo had come with ten of their helpers to assist, and by the end of three days everything had been carried up.

Now, at last, there were plenty of drugs and bandages,

but until the promised building should be put up it was very difficult to find a place in which to store everything. The industrial[1] missionary put up a few shelves in the Doctor's little sitting-room on which some of the drugs could be stored for the time being, but that was all. Worse than anything, there was no building at all in which to receive and examine patients. It all had to be done in the open air. Remembering the Schweitzer Hospital as it is to-day, forty years later, with its forty separate buildings, we cannot but be amazed at the small beginning from which it has grown.

The patients were waiting, and the Doctor had to make some arrangements for them. It was very exhausting work treating them in the open air in that hot tropical climate. He noticed a small fowlhouse which had been used as such by the missionary who had formerly lived in his bungalow, and decided to use it as his hospital building. There was only room in it for a camp-bed and a few medicines, but still it was better than nothing.

His wife was the first nurse to help him in his work, and, besides keeping house, she used to come for several hours a day to assist with the patients. An intelligent African named Joseph was soon discovered among the patients. He could speak some French, the language used on the mission station, and so could act as an interpreter as well as a helper. So Joseph was engaged as such, and very useful he became. In time he was able to help with the bandaging and even gave out medicines without mistaking one for another.

So here we have the beginnings of the Schweitzer Hospital of to-day—one doctor, one nurse, one African helper, and a fowlhouse for a hospital.

[1]There is very often an *industrial* missionary at a mission school to teach manual work or do manual jobs.

CHAPTER FIVE

THE HOSPITAL GROWS

THE Africans were delighted with their new doctor and came in great numbers to the fowlhouse hospital to be treated.

Every morning the Doctor's six rules were read out in the languages of the two chief tribes, the Galoas and the Pahouins. Among the rules were some ordering, "No spitting near the Doctor's house," "No loud talking," "Enough food for the day to be brought." This last was necessary, as there were often so many patients waiting that some of them could not be seen until the evening.

The Doctor from the outset kept a very methodical register of all his patients, their names, their complaints, and all the bottles, bandages, and other things given out, so that he could ask for them back again. There was a number put against each patient in the Doctor's register, and when each left after treatment he was given a cardboard disc with the number written on it. This was usually hung round the patient's neck with a piece of fibre, and there was very little danger of his losing or forgetting it, as it was regarded as a sort of fetish or charm given by the white doctor. Sometimes the patients were given medicine to be taken in doses, sometimes pills, sometimes ointment to rub on, but though Joseph did his best to interpret the Doctor's instructions (given in French) into the various African languages one could never be quite sure whether they might not eat the ointment or drink the whole bottle of medicine at a draught.

As time went on Joseph began to make himself very useful, even in making up the medicines. He got to know the most ordinary ones by the look of the bottle.

One thing which caused a great deal of extra work was the irresponsibility and unreliability of the Africans. They are rather like little children, who have to be taught that they must not take what does not belong to them. This idea was foreign to them in a way, because in the forest everything is free and open. As Joseph himself said, whatever is left unattended "goes for a walk." This meant for the doctor constant journeys back and forth from the fowlhouse to the bungalow to fetch this or that medicine as it was needed. The Africans do not at all resent the fact that everything has to be locked up away from them; on the contrary they sometimes insist on it, because, then, if anything is lost they cannot be accused of taking it.

After about two and a half months' work in the fowl-house hospital the missionaries told Dr Schweitzer that there was going to be a conference at Samkita, some thirty miles away by canoe, and it would be a good opportunity for him to put his case, and see whether anything could be done about erecting the hospital building which he had been promised.

So two hours before daybreak one morning two missionaries and the Doctor set off, rowed by a crew of twelve. It took them more than twelve hours to go up-stream even this short distance, and they took camp-bedsteads with them and food, and also boxes and tins in which to bring back some stores from Samkita.

They were very kindly greeted at the conference, and it was decided that the corrugated-iron building and other small buildings might be put up at the bottom of the hill on which the Doctor's bungalow was. He was also given eighty pounds in money towards the cost of building. They returned home with joyful and thankful hearts.

The next thing was to try to recruit some African labourers to help in levelling the site. After a little while about a dozen were found, and the site was chosen. Dr Schweitzer himself took a spade and helped in this work, and after two days the ground was ready for the buildings to be erected on it.

Now there was another delay, for the Doctor was suddenly called away to attend to a case of sunstroke at N'Gomo. When he returned he found to his great joy that the hospital building was finished; it had been put up by the industrial workers at the mission during his absence. It had two rooms, each thirteen feet square, one for a consulting-room and one for an operating-theatre, and also two smaller rooms for dispensary and sterilizing-room. So now the fowlhouse which for some months had been the only hospital could be left behind. The new rooms had cement floors and large windows going right up to the roof, which added to the coolness of the building. There was no glass in the windows but very fine mosquito-proof wire-netting, and wooden shutters. White calico was stretched under the roof to keep out any mosquitoes which might have found their way in through holes. Round the walls were placed the great blessings of wide shelves.

The Schweitzer hospital was growing. There was still, however, no room for beds—what we should call a ward for patients who had to remain at the hospital. However, during the next month, December, one was built by the Doctor himself with other helpers. You may wonder how the Doctor could set to and build a ward. You must not imagine a ward such as the wards in an

English hospital. This ward was just built of logs, with raffia leaves for a roof like those of the African huts. The sides would be open to the air. What about beds? That problem was quickly and inexpensively solved. As soon as the roof was on Dr Schweitzer went inside with a pointed stick, and on the floor of beaten earth he marked out sixteen large oblongs, with paths between. Then he sent for the patients (who in the meantime had been accommodated in a boathouse) and put one patient into each of the oblongs. To each of the friends who accompanied the patients he gave an axe and told him to make a bed. To an African this would be quite natural. Off they went in their canoes, up-stream and down-stream, to fetch wood. Four short forked sticks placed one at each corner and planted in the earthen floor, two side poles and two cross poles fixed into the forks, all bound firmly together with strong stalks of creepers—this makes a bed. With some dried grass for mattresses the beds are ready for the patients, and not one has cost anyone a penny. There is also room under the beds to store boxes, food, and other things. The beds are wide so that the patients' friends may sleep with them if they wish; if not they sleep on the floor on a mat which they will bring with them. Dr Schweitzer had to make one rule, and that was that the friends must not put the patients on the floor and use the beds themselves!

Besides this ward, a waiting-room was built, and a little room for Joseph.

With the erection of the iron building and the patients' ward and waiting-room, the hospital grew apace. As it was at the water's edge, most of the patients arrived in canoes brought by their friends from up-stream and down-stream, sometimes from a distance of over two hundred miles.

Joseph became a very reliable assistant, and was able to be left in charge sometimes when the Doctor had to be elsewhere. The Doctor's wife gave invaluable help in many ways, administering the anæsthetics before an operation and boiling and sterilizing the instruments and bandages afterwards. It took the Africans a long time to realize that this sterilizing was necessary. They were, however, very much impressed by the anæsthetics which the Doctor, helped by his wife, administered when they performed an operation. One African girl wrote a letter to another girl in a Sunday school in Europe and said: "Since the Doctor has been here we have seen the most wonderful things happen. First he kills the patients, then he cures them, and then he brings them to life again."

The Africans often have terrible illnesses of which we in Europe know very little—malaria, leprosy, sleeping-sickness, and also large sores and ulcers which go right down to the bone.

It was a great trouble to Dr Schweitzer that he had no room in the hospital which he could use for sleeping-sickness patients, so that they should not spread the infection among the rest. This illness is carried by both mosquitoes and tsetse-flies from an infected person to a healthy person. In order to find out whether a person is suffering from sleeping-sickness the blood has to be carefully examined, and this can take up the best part of a whole morning while the other patients are clamouring impatiently for treatment.

As time went on the Doctor was able to have a small hut erected on the other side of the river especially for these patients. That was a great weight off his mind, but, of course, it entailed a great deal of extra work. There certainly was no lack of that. How Dr Schweitzer began to long for another doctor to help him! But how

A dormitory at the Schweitzer hospital, where patients come with members of their families, their goats, and their belongings

Dr Schweitzer and his carpenter

glad he was that he himself had come there to be of use!
He has told us in his book *On the Edge of the Primeval
Forest*[1] a story of one of his black patients on whom he
had performed a successful operation.

> The operation is finished, and in the hardly lighted
> dormitory I watch for the sick man's awakening. Scarcely
> has he recovered consciousness when he stares about him
> and ejaculates again and again: "I've no more pain! I've
> no more pain!" . . . His hand feels for mine and will not
> let it go. Then I begin to tell him and the others who are in
> the room that it is the Lord Jesus who has told the doctor
> and his wife to come to the Ogowe, and that white people
> in Europe give them the money to live here and cure the
> sick Negroes. Then I have to answer questions as to who
> these white people are, where they live, and how they know
> that the natives suffer from so much sickness. The African
> sun is shining through the coffee-bushes into the dark shed,
> but we, black and white, sit side by side and feel that we
> know by experience the meaning of the words: "And all
> ye are brethren." (Matt. xxiii, 8.)

It was for this that Schweitzer had given up all his fame
and honours in Europe, and he felt amply rewarded.

There came a time when the Doctor himself had to
be treated for an abscess, and he and his wife went down
to Cape Lopez to consult the military doctor there.
They stayed for a short time while he was convalescent
at the house of a factory employee, and, as he was not
allowed to work, he used to sit out in a deck-chair on
the veranda. It was a pleasant time of refreshment, as
there were sea-breezes there, a contrast to the atmosphere
at Lambaréné; and, in order not to be idle, the Doctor
occupied the time in writing about the timber-trade as
carried on there. About one hundred and fifty thousand

[1] Published by A. and C. Black (1953).

D

tons of timber a year were being exported at the time the
doctor was writing (1914), magnificent trunks of mahogany and other trees which had been felled in the forest
miles up-stream and brought down to Cape Lopez in
the form of rafts. If a tree is to be cut down in England
a few hours will suffice for the trunk to fall, and a few
more for the cutting up, but the trees in Equatorial
Africa are so huge that often they cannot begin to be
sawn through for the distance of six or seven feet above
the ground. Several days' work is necessary before the
tree is ready to fall, and when it has fallen the huge trunk
and boughs have to be cut up into pieces of varying
length and thickness. After that the great pieces, which
may weigh anything up to three tons, have to be rolled
over and over to the place where they will be ready to be
floated off when the high water comes up in November
or December. Any tree-trunk which misses this high
tide has to stay where it is, and so the work is wasted.

When the trunks have reached the water a number of
them, up to a hundred perhaps, will be bound together
by strong creepers from the forest to make a raft, and
this will be floated down the river with a crew on board.
It may take a fortnight to travel down the river to Cape
Lopez, and even then if a storm should get up the raft
may be swept out to sea and lost.

At Cape Lopez the raft is taken to pieces and put into
a 'park,' from which the ship will fetch the logs in due
course.

This is the work for which the timber-traders are so
anxious to obtain the African's labour, and so are willing
to pay him larger wages than the missionaries or the
Doctor are able to do.

After a week or so the Doctor's convalescence was
complete, and he and his wife travelled back again to

Lambaréné on a little steamer which happened to be going there. It was now about fifteen months since they had first arrived, and much had been accomplished in that time.

They arrived back on August 2 from Cape Lopez, and just two days after their arrival a sad thing happened.

CHAPTER SIX

WAR

ON August 5 Joseph was sent to the store at Lambaréné to buy some medicine for a lady who was ill at Cape Lopez. The storekeeper was asked to send the medicine down by the next river-steamer, but instead of saying, "Yes, certainly I will," he took a piece of paper and wrote on it a short note, which he gave to Joseph, telling him to show it to the Doctor.

The note read: "In Europe they are mobilizing and probably already at war. We must place our steamer at the disposal of the authorities and cannot tell when it will go next to Cape Lopez."

This was the beginning of the First World War, which was to last four years and a quarter.

The Doctor and his wife were really German citizens, because Alsace had belonged to Germany since the Franco-Prussian War in 1870, and so in theory they and the Paris Missionary Society with whom he was working were in opposite camps. That very evening they were informed by those responsible for the government of this French colony that they were prisoners of war. They might for the present continue to stay on in their little house, but must not speak to or hold communication with any person, white or black.

The Africans could not understand that the white men (represented to them by the doctor and the missionaries) who had brought them a gospel of love should be fighting among themselves. War seemed a very far-away thing out here in the primeval forest.

"Ten men killed already!" exclaimed an old warrior, belonging to the Pahouin cannibal tribe. "Why don't the tribes (meaning the Europeans) get together for a big palaver and settle things? How can they pay for all these dead men?" It is a custom in tribal warfare that every man killed must be paid for by the opposite side, quite apart from the question of which side eventually wins the war, and to this old African ten men already killed seemed a tremendous number.[1]

The Doctor now had all his time to himself since he was forbidden to work in the hospital, but he never liked to be idle. Before he came out to Africa he had been in the middle of writing a book about St Paul, and he also had in his head thoughts and ideas about another book on civilization in general.

Now, he thought to himself, when the fact of the War has proved that we are not so civilized as we thought we were, this is the time to write this book.

So, morning after morning, after breakfast he sat down at the writing-table in his little study and wrote some pages of this large book, which he hoped would be published some day.

After about three months the news was brought that the Doctor was free to work in the hospital again. He had his friend Widor, the French organist, to thank for this.

It was a great pleasure to both the black and the white people at Lambaréné to have their doctor again working among them. He was the only doctor for miles around, and they had all been very indignant at his being unable to continue helping them, just because Germany happened to be fighting France miles away.

On the first Christmas Day after the outbreak of war

[1] From *On the Edge of the Primeval Forest*.

the Doctor and his wife had a little palm-tree instead of the Christmas-tree they would have had in their own Alsatian village. When the candles were half burnt down on it the Doctor blew them out. "They are all we have," he said, "and we must keep them for next year."

Although he was now busy again with the hospital, he found a little time each evening to continue writing his great book *The Philosophy of Civilization*. It was a very deep book indeed, for Schweitzer was a very deep thinker. He had got to a part of the book which puzzled him. He did not seem to be able to get on any further with it until he had decided for himself what exactly he meant by 'civilization.' He knew clearly in his own mind more or less what he meant, but he could not coin a phrase which would convey what he meant to other people.

One day in the summer of the next year, 1915, he was staying for a little time at Cape Lopez for the sake of his wife's health, and during the visit he had to make a journey up-stream to visit a missionary's wife who was ill. As he was travelling up the familiar river hour after hour his mind was still vaguely thinking about his book. Suddenly some words flashed into his mind: "Reverence for Life."

"That's what I mean. That's the wording which will express what I mean by civilization," he thought to himself. The problem was solved.

Reverence for Life! That meant care and consideration for every one. That was what made people civilized, and it all fitted in with Christianity and the love of Jesus.

Reverence for Life! Care and consideration for all, big or small, and not only for people but for animals too, even the tiniest of them. They want to live just as much as we do, he thought. He remembered how when he was quite a little boy he had always been surprised that people only said prayers for other people and not for animals, and how he had invented a little prayer for animals which he used himself every night.

Yes, the life of animals to themselves was as important as our lives are to ourselves. He put it like this in his language of philosophy: "I am life which wills to live in the midst of life which wills to live."

As he began to think more deeply about it he realized how difficult it was to decide exactly to what this "Reverence for Life" brought one. It meant firstly that one must not kill any living creature without a good reason. Sometimes it was hard to decide what was a good reason. For instance, he had once rescued a little fish-eagle from some Africans who were ill-treating it, and, having rescued it, of course he had to feed it. As the natural food of this little bird was fish, he had either to let it starve or to kill every day several small fish to feed it. In the long run he decided to do this, but he realized that it is almost always a choice between two things. It was clear to him that there is never any hard-and-fast rule in the matter and that every one has to decide for himself on each occasion. But, he went on to think, if it is necessary sometimes to take life, it is possible sometimes to pay it back, so to speak, in another way. For instance, if he found a little ant struggling on its back in the middle of the path or a worm lying where it might be trodden on he would take the trouble to stoop down and move them to a place of safety. The same thing applies to our relations with one another. If every one of us does a little according to his ability to relieve the suffering in the world, at any rate some little part of it will be brought to an end.

When Dr Schweitzer had first decided to give his life

to Africa people used to come to visit him and ask him whether they also ought to give up whatever they were doing and do as he had done. His answer was: "Only a person who can find a value in every sort of activity and devote himself to each one with full consciousness of duty has the inward right to take as his object some extraordinary activity instead of that which falls naturally to his lot."[1]

By this he meant to say that very often our ordinary day-to-day work is the right work for us, and we must not think that because it is sometimes dull or monotonous it is a waste of our abilities and time and that we ought to be doing something bigger and more spectacular, and which will bring us more into the limelight. Schweitzer himself did exactly the opposite. He was already in the limelight, famous for his music, his books, his preaching, his lecturing, and he chose to give it all up and go out to serve in a mission which most of his friends would probably never even have heard of. He did not expect praise; he had the disapproval of many whose opinion he valued, but he went away quietly, even with sadness, and with no heroic feelings. He was even prepared for the hardest thing of all—that the plan for which he had laboured so hard and long might be a failure. It was but an experiment, but he felt that he was strong enough to bear the consequences even if it should fail and people should turn round and say: "I told you so."

When later on it turned to success he gave thanks to God for it.

So he went on doing his work and writing his great book. A year went by, and it was Christmas time again, Christmas 1915. The candle-ends saved from last year's

[1] From *My Life and Thought*.

palm Christmas-tree were used again, but there was nothing left of them for another year. Sometimes he would give himself the pleasure of a little music. Music? On the edge of the primeval forest? Yes, and not radio music either, but music which he played himself on the piano with the pedal-attachments which the Paris Bach Society had given him when he came to Africa. It had been a wonderful comfort to him now that he had no real church organ to play upon, and here in the depths of the solitude of Africa he was able to solace himself by playing the music of his favourite composer, Bach.

The money which had formerly been so generously collected and sent to the Doctor by his many European friends for the hospital now began to run short—no more was coming. To his great grief he had to put the faithful Joseph, who had served the hospital well for two and a half years, on half-pay. The result was that Joseph decided to leave the Doctor's service—for the time being. There was another African helper besides, but he could not do all the things Joseph had been able to do, so that more responsibility fell upon the Doctor and his wife.

They were both getting very tired, and, of course, there was no question of a furlough.

Another Christmas came—Christmas 1916. There were no candles for the palm Christmas-tree this year.

News of the War only reached Lambaréné once a fortnight; it was telegraphed to the store, and African soldiers brought it up to the mission station. The months went on, and suddenly, in September 1917, when the War was just over three years old, an order came that the Doctor and his wife were to leave Africa at once and be interned in a prisoner-of-war camp in Europe.

Every one was sorry to see them go. The Father Superior of the Roman Catholic Mission came on board just before they sailed to shake hands and say good-bye, and thank them for all the good work that they had done.

Everything, including the precious piano with the organ pedal-attachments, had to be left behind. Not even the pages of the book the Doctor was writing could be taken. One of the missionaries promised to look after this, and the doctor made a quick summary of it in French to take with him.

He managed, however, to take some of his Bach music with him, and on the homeward journey on board ship, where he was allowed to speak to no one, he played the music silently with his fingers on the bare table, and moved his feet on the floor as if feeling for organ pedals. In this way, without any real instrument, he learnt several of Bach's compositions by heart.

One of his old patients had especially come before-hand to speak to the steward on the boat and ask him to treat the Doctor well, and so the steward did his best for him. His 'gaoler' at the internment camp also showed him kindness. Nobody had any personal complaints against him; it was just a political necessity.

He must have felt as if all his years of work at the hospital had been wasted.

But the end of the Schweitzer hospital on the edge of the primeval forest had not come yet.

CHAPTER SEVEN

IN EUROPE AGAIN

D R SCHWEITZER and his wife were taken first to an internment camp at a place called Garaison. At first they did not allow him to practise there as a doctor, though later they were pleased for him to do so. So during the time when he had nothing in particular to do he spent his time continuing to write his great book *The Philosophy of Civilization*, and in practising his organ-music silently on table and floor as he had done on the boat. One of the other prisoners of war drew a very amusing caricature of the Doctor engaged in doing this so energetically that the cups and plates were dancing off the table on to the floor. The Doctor, who always found a silver lining to every cloud, found a pleasure here in the number of men of different walks of life whom he met among the prisoners—architects, bankers, builders, cereal-growers, and others—from whom he picked up many valuable hints.

In March of the next year he and his wife were transferred to another camp which was for Alsatians only, and in July of the same year to their great joy an exchange of prisoners was arranged and they were allowed to go, via Switzerland, home again. Mme Schweitzer went first to her parents and the doctor to the dear little village of Günsbach.

It was a very different Günsbach from the peaceful one they had left five years before. Now there were barbed-wire entanglements in the quiet valley, gun emplacements, and black-outs.

The Doctor and his wife were both in bad health, so much so that in September he had to undergo an operation. When he had recovered his strength a little he had to consider seriously the question of finding some means of earning a living. The Mayor of Strasburg soon offered him a post as one of the doctors at the Municipal Hospital in that city.

You will not have forgotten that he used to preach and teach as curate of St Nicholas's Church, Strasburg, before going to Africa, and this was one of the things he had most regretted having to give up. Now this post was offered to him again, and he and his wife came to live in Strasburg, where, at the beginning of the next year, January 14, 1919, a little daughter was born to them. They named her Rhena.

Meantime, on November 11 of the previous year, the Armistice had been signed, and the First World War had come to an end. Alsace became a French possession, and so the Schweitzers and other Alsatians became French subjects instead of Germans.

About Christmas-time 1919 the Doctor received an unexpected but very welcome invitation. It came from Sweden, from Archbishop Söderblom, and it was to ask him to deliver a course of lectures next Easter at the Swedish University of Upsala. It pleased the Doctor very much to find that he was still remembered in Europe; he had begun to feel, as he said, "like a coin that has rolled under a piece of furniture and been forgotten."

He accepted the Archbishop's invitation gratefully, though still tired and far from well. He and his wife travelled together to Sweden (leaving little Rhena, we must imagine, with some of her aunts or grandparents) and stayed with the Archbishop as his guests. The fine air of Sweden and the kindness they received completely set them up again in health.

One great worry the Doctor had and could not get rid of was the thought of all the debts he had had to leave behind when he left Africa so suddenly as a prisoner of war. One day, as they were sharing an umbrella during a shower of rain, he discussed this with the kindly Archbishop, who suggested that Schweitzer should travel round to some of the larger cities in Sweden, giving lectures and also organ recitals (for, thanks to the persevering practice on the piano with the pedal-attachments in Africa, and also on the table and floor afterwards, he was still a competent organist).

This plan exactly suited the Doctor. But, although he spoke fluent French and fluent German, he had never studied the Swedish language, and so there had to be an interpreter. Of course, to interpret an entire lecture lasting perhaps an hour would be a very different matter from Joseph's interpreting at Lambaréné to tell the natives how their medicines should be taken. Fortunately, an excellent interpreter was found, a young Swedish gentleman, and he and the Doctor rehearsed the lecture together beforehand.

The Archbishop's plan was very successful, and Schweitzer had a very happy time, creating much interest in his hospital and making many friends. In a few weeks he had made enough money to pay off a good many of the debts.

Now that he felt stronger his thoughts began turning again to his hospital, which occupied a very large part of his heart, and he began to wonder whether it would be possible to go back there and take up his work again. It was about this time that one of the best known of his books was published, the one about his hospital and

called *On the Edge of the Primeval Forest*. It appeared
in Swedish, in Dutch, German, Danish, French,
Finnish, English, and Spanish.

In April 1921 he thought he could now make enough
money by writing books and giving organ recitals, so
he gave up his two posts as doctor and as curate in
Strasburg and settled down quietly with his wife and
little daughter Rhena, two years old now, in the old
parsonage in Günsbach, where he had spent his childhood. Here he continued writing his big book *The
Philosophy of Civilization*, and in 1923 the first two
volumes were published. There still remained a third
volume which he hoped to complete later. During these
years also he visited England and gave lectures at Oxford,
Birmingham, Cambridge, and London, making many
friends in this country. Before he could leave for Africa
again he had to accumulate a sum of money to keep his
wife and little girl while he was away, because he knew
that Mme Schweitzer would not be able to accompany
him this time.

He felt full of gratitude to her for allowing him to
return. "Unceasingly I thank her in my heart," he
wrote, "that she rose to the sacrifice of acquiescence in
my return under these circumstances to Lambaréné."

He also felt full of gratitude to the people of Alsace,
Switzerland, Sweden, Denmark, England, and Czechoslovakia for the money they had subscribed in answer
to the appeal put forth in his lectures.

He was to leave his home for Africa on February 21,
1924, and he spent the last evening before he left in
dedicating a new little organ (built to his own design)
in the church at Mühlbach where his grandfather
Schillinger, his mother's father, had been pastor. Their
church and organ had been destroyed during the War.

There is not room in this story to tell much about Dr Schweitzer and his organs, but we ought to know that, besides being an exceptional organist, he has also learnt to understand how to build organs, and what sort of organs are best. He likes the old organs better than modern factory-made ones, especially for the music of his favourite composer, Bach. It has been said of him: "In Africa he saves old niggers; in Europe he saves old organs." He has travelled round inspecting many and many an organ which has almost come to the end of its life, and trying to persuade those responsible to have the old organ restored rather than have a new one. On one occasion he was to preach in a church in Holland on Christmas Day. Christmas Day was a Saturday, and he arrived the Monday before, but, except at mealtimes, hardly anything was seen of him, and it was wondered what he was doing.

At last he was discovered up in the organ loft of the church, hot and dusty, clearing the organ-pipes of all the dirt that had for years collected round them.

When Christmas Day came he not only preached the sermon but played the organ, and so beautifully that the people exclaimed in amazement: "Is that our old organ?"

And so he spent his last evening before sailing for Africa in dedicating the new Mühlbach organ.

"I first played in this church as a nine-year-old boy," he told the people.

"My grandfather Schillinger had built a fine organ under the direction of the organ-builder, Stier. How happy I was before my first journey to Africa to restore it. Then in the primeval forest I read in a Swiss paper that not merely the organ but the Church and the pastor's house, indeed the whole village had been destroyed in a barrage. It seemed as if my heart would break. The next day I met a Negro king who lived across the river from me in Lambaréné and he said to me: 'Oganga' (one of the nicknames bestowed by the natives) 'Why are you so sad?' I said: 'In my homeland they have destroyed things that are beautiful and dear to me. There was an organ among them.' And the King asked: 'What is that, an organ?' I had difficulty in explaining to him what an organ was. . . . . Then I asked him: 'King, will you give me the beautiful mahogany tree that stands there on the bank of the river, spreading out in such majesty?' 'Yes,' he said, 'I will give this to you for the organ in your homeland.' How I thanked him when I thought of you, dear homeless people. I had men come to fell the tree and saw it up into boards by hand—there is no other way of doing this in Lambaréné; and had the boards placed under a roof and planned to sell them for you when they were dry."[1]

He went on to explain that while he was a prisoner the beautiful boards had rotted away. But later, when he was in London, he had been allowed to give a concert in a church and devote the money to a new organ for Mühlbach—this new organ which he was now dedicating. He played to them for an hour some of his favourite music—Bach, Mendelssohn, Widor.

Then he left them.

The next day he started on his second journey to Africa.

[1] From *Music in the Life of Albert Schweitzer*, by C. Joy, published by A. and C. Black (1953).

A scene in the hospital, where Dr Schweitzer has planned the buildings so as to get the maximum coolness

Dr Schweitzer with two of his antelopes

From "The Africa of Albert Schweitzer" (A. and C. Black), by C. R. Joy and M. Arnold

CHAPTER EIGHT

RETURN TO LAMBARÉNÉ

IT was on February 14, 1924, that Dr Schweitzer started on his second journey to Lambaréné, nearly eleven years since he had started with his wife for the first time.

During these eleven years the hospital had made friends in almost every European country, with the result that the Doctor had to deal with an immense amount of correspondence. He carried this with him in four large potato-sacks, thinking that the voyage would give him an opportunity of getting rid of some of it. When he had to pass through the Customs office at Bordeaux the Customs officer was rather puzzled and slightly suspicious. He could not understand why any-one should want to take away all these letters addressed to himself, and thought there must be gold or banknotes in them. It was strictly forbidden at this time in France for gold to leave the country. The officer spent an hour and a half opening one letter after another, but when he came to the bottom of the second sack he decided to give it up and let them pass.

Although Mme Schweitzer had not been able to accompany her husband on this occasion, he was not alone. He had as a companion a young Oxford under-graduate, aged eighteen, named Nöel Gillespie, who was going to give his services for several months.

They purposely travelled on a cargo-boat, so that they would have an opportunity of stopping at places on the way.

E

There was only one other passenger on the boat, a lady, and during the voyage a little baby was born to her. As there was no one else on board who had time to look after her, Dr Schweitzer did so, and young Nöel Gillespie looked after the baby, going eight times a day to the galley in the sweltering tropical heat to prepare its bottles.

In due course they arrived at Cape Lopez, as on the former journey, eleven years ago, and on the beach there the Doctor was recognized with great joy by some of the Africans who had known him in the earlier days. They pursued their way up the Ogowe river in the *Alembe*, the very same river-boat on which the Doctor had made the journey in 1913, but she was much older and dirtier now.

It was Good Friday 1924 when they drew near to the familiar scenes at Lambaréné, and at sunrise on Easter Eve (April 19) they had arrived. The journey had taken longer than on the previous occasion, as they had stopped a fortnight on the way.

After they had reached Lambaréné there followed the last stage of the journey in the dug-out canoe, and soon the three familiar hills of the mission station came in sight, and the canoe drew to the shore. Nöel superintended the unloading of the luggage, while the Doctor went on, full of eagerness to see his beloved hospital again after his seven years' absence.

He has himself described this scene. "I walk up to the hospital," he says,

> like one in a dream. It might be the Sleeping Beauty's place of concealment! Grass and brushwood are growing where once stood the wards which I constructed with so much trouble. Above what is still standing are stretched the boughs of big trees which I remember as little saplings.

There are still standing the building of corrugated iron in which we had our operating-room, consulting-room, and dispensary, and another in which we housed some of the patients. These two are in fairly good condition, though their roofs of palm-leaves are hopelessly damaged. The path from the hospital to the little Doctor's house on the hill is so overgrown with grass that I can scarcely follow its windings."[1]

But the French missionaries were there, as friendly as ever. They had tried to keep the roof in repair, but had had to give up the attempt, as there were no more stitched leaf-tiles to be had. All the Africans whose work it had formerly been to make them had been drawn away to cut timber in the forest for the timber-merchants, who had enormous orders for it for two international exhibitions in Europe and in America.

Owing to the holes in the leaf-roof, nothing could be stored in the hospital until it was mended.

In spite of what must have been to him a bitter disappointment, the Doctor characteristically made up his mind at once what must be done.

They had only arrived about midday, and had just had lunch with the missionaries, but by three o'clock the Doctor, with Nöel, was setting off in a canoe to go to a village about an hour and a half's journey away to see if any leaf-tiles could be procured there.

The Africans of this village knew him well, and were delighted to greet him. From hut to hut he went, searching for leaf-tiles. At last, after much persuasion and giving of presents, sixty-four tiles were secured, and with these the Doctor and Nöel returned in their canoe in pouring rain to mend the worst holes. To cover the entire roof they would need three thousand.

The Doctor walked again up the overgrown path to

[1] *More from the Primeval Forest*, A. and C. Black (1931).

his little bungalow. One of the missionaries was occupying two of the rooms, and a swarm of bees had settled in a third, but there was still one for the Doctor and Nöel.

Sad he was and disappointed, but as usual he made the best of it, and said that he could now "keep Easter with a contented mind."

Next day, Easter Monday, the first patients began to arrive, and at the same time the repairing of the hospital had to begin. The Doctor managed to get a half dozen African labourers to help him, and sometimes they were able to work alone while he looked after his patients and unpacked his medicines.

Many a precious afternoon did he or Nöel have to spend in going on canoe journeys in search of stitched leaf-tiles for the roofs, or for big bamboo-canes, which only grew in certain swampy places, or bark from special trees which is made into the cord to bind the bamboos and the walls and the leaf-tiles together. Sometimes he would threaten not to give treatment to patients except in exchange for leaf-tiles, but the Africans did not take this seriously, and the Doctor was too kind-hearted to insist upon it.

Nöel made himself wonderfully useful in a great variety of ways. He and the Doctor had to do practically all the work, both of doctoring and of building, though at one time and another they were able to get a little help from Africans. An African will work very hard indeed for one of his own tribe, but does not understand the idea of helping some one he does not know.

Nöel very quickly learnt to help in giving the injections to patients suffering from sleeping-sickness or deep-seated ulcers, and, as there might be as many as twenty of these injections to be given in a day, this was a very great relief to the Doctor. Nöel was also responsible for filling the lamps, boiling the drinking-water, doing the washing, and looking after the fowls. One day the fowl-house floor collapsed under his feet, and, as the wood was too rotten to be mended, a new fowlhouse had very quickly to be put together, for the leopards would soon have destroyed any fowls which were at large by night. This work was done by Nöel, and he also constructed a strong kind of cell for a patient who had become very wild and dangerous as a result of sleeping-sickness. This is a very common result of the disease, but it is usually only temporary. This patient completely recovered later on, and as he had no home he stayed on and became useful at the hospital.

The husband of another sleeping-sickness patient was found to have a knowledge of carpentry, and he also helped the doctor in the rebuilding. His name was Monenzalie, and he is still there and giving help thirty years afterwards.

On July 18 a wonderful thing happened. A nurse arrived from Strasburg to help. Her name was Mlle Kottmann, and she is also still helping the hospital.

Some of the African timber-merchants collected a sum of money to present to the Doctor towards Nurse Kottmann's fare, which pleased him very much.

Almost at the same time Joseph, who had been the Doctor's original "first assistant" in 1913, came back again to help. He had a wife now, and was in the timber-trade, so it was not certain how long he would remain at the hospital, but in any case his help was very welcome at the present time.

But now in August they had to say good-bye to Nöel, whose time in Africa was up. He had helped so capably in such a number of ways that the doctor hardly knew how to thank sufficiently "this good comrade" as he calls him. But Nöel had to go back to his university life at Oxford, and the Doctor pictures how, amid his lectures, he will look back as in a dream to his months in Africa when he was 'doctor's assistant,' carpenter, foreman, sexton, and other things besides.

On October 19 one of the Doctor's dearest wishes came true at last, and that was that he should have another doctor to help him in his work and to share all the responsibility which the running of the hospital as well as other things placed upon him. A new young doctor, Dr Nessman, whose father had known Dr Schweitzer in Strasburg, arrived. The Africans used to call Dr Schweitzer "Le Grand Docteur," meaning the chief doctor, and now they called Dr Nessman "Le Petit Docteur," because he was young.

Dr Schweitzer was now able to give up much of his work with the patients to 'le Petit Docteur,' while he himself organized the rebuilding and repairing. He wanted to make movable beds out of hardwood which could be taken out into the sun and cleaned when necessary, and also, to save room, he planned to build beds one above the other, like bunks in a ship.

At last forty beds were ready, and then some storerooms were begun, and another ward to hold thirty beds. Also a new little house was to be built for the 'little' doctor, who was at present living with the missionaries. However much was done, there always seemed to be something more which needed doing.

At New Year 1925 the 'old' doctor, the 'little' doctor, and Nurse Kottmann were all out of sorts. One had boils, one had ulcers on the feet, and one just felt 'done up.' Dr Schweitzer, who was the one with ulcers on his feet, managed to drag himself about somehow and do what he could.

How encouraging then was the news that a third doctor was on the way—Dr Lauterburg of Berne.

The work at the hospital had so much increased from its small beginnings that now even two doctors could not really cope with it. Besides the treatment of illnesses and sores and other complaints, there were quite a number of operations to be performed. How welcome a third doctor would be! And another nurse was coming too. All this, of course, meant more rooms to be built.

The Doctor found a piece of vacant land on the mission station and determined to build there a ward sixty feet by twenty feet, with ten rooms in it, for white patients, for there were quite a number of these who began to come to the Schweitzer hospital, originally built for black patients only. So the scope of the hospital was being gradually enlarged.

When Dr Lauterburg arrived the Africans were not long in giving him a nickname. It was 'N'Tschinda N'Tschinda'—the man who cuts boldly. This was because Dr Lauterburg, if he saw a badly poisoned arm or leg, generally amputated it, to save the poison from spreading to the rest of the body.

That time was really what we call a 'chapter of good news,' for besides the arrival of the second nurse and of 'N'Tschinda N'Tschinda,' a young Swiss, named Monsieur Schatzmann, offered his help in building. The Schweitzer hospital was becoming widely known in other countries, and it had many friends anxious to help.

Another much needed thing arrived as a present from Sweden, where Dr Schweitzer had given organ recitals and lectures to get money for his second journey to Africa in 1924. This present was a beautiful motorboat, which would do journeys up and down the river far more speedily than the canoes could.

During the summer the Doctor managed to get his own bungalow reroofed with leaf-tiles; but in the middle of September the rains set in, and some of the roofs began to leak again.

It had always been a great trouble to obtain the leaf-tiles, and many presents had to be given to the Africans in exchange for them. Even so, they only lasted for about three years and needed constant attention.

The Doctor thought the question over, and then made a decision. He would give up leaf-tile roofs entirely and make his roofs of corrugated iron instead. Once he had made the decision there was no more change of mind.

In the next order which he sent to Europe by the down-river steamer he ordered to be sent out by the next ship several hundred square yards of corrugated iron.

CHAPTER NINE

THE HOSPITAL MAKES A MOVE

AFTER the Doctor had made his decision about the corrugated-iron roofs and dispatched his order to Europe the hospital had to go on as usual until the corrugated iron should arrive.

But there was always something unexpected waiting round the corner. In the autumn of 1925 came an enemy in the shape of famine. The chief foods of the native African were bananas and manioc (a kind of tapioca in thick sticks), and there had been a shortage of these for some time. However, the shortage had been partly made up for by large imports of rice from Europe. But there was not enough, and of what there was one whole shipment had been lost in a wreck.

So famine began to stare the district in the face. The hospital fared fairly well, since they had laid in stores some time earlier, but the timber-traders and others had begun to feel the pinch of want.

Added to this there was a severe outbreak of dysentery among the African patients, and a rice diet was not good for this complaint. The doctor could face his hardships mostly with courage and calmness, but it troubled and discouraged him sorely that he had no building in which he could isolate his dysentery patients to prevent the disease from spreading. The native Africans have little or no idea of the spreading of a disease through germs, as we have. To them most illnesses are caused through magic, or by spells cast by some one who wishes them ill. They would in kindness of heart share food and drink

with their friends suffering from disease, with the result
that it would spread and could not be stamped out.

In the middle of October, however, came a very
welcome arrival in the person of Mlle Emma Hausknecht,
an old friend of the Doctor's, who had promised him a
long while ago that she would come to help and now at
last found it possible to do so. She would be able to help
in the nursing and do other things besides. It was in
1925 that Mlle Hausknecht came, and if you were to go
out to the Schweitzer Hospital at the present time,
thirty years later, you would find her still there, and
taking a tremendous amount of the hospital's responsibility upon her shoulders. When she first arrived she
was able to undertake the housekeeping, as the Doctor's
wife had done during his first sojourn in Africa. She
also looked after the white patients, of whom quite a
number were always found in the hospital Dr Schweitzer
had built for the Africans.

Nurse Kottmann then could give her attention to the
African patients and also—what no other European
nurse would undertake to do—give out the rations, keep
the fires going, give out tools for the forest work, keep
an eye on the canoes, and, last but not least, settle all
the disputes in the hospital.

With two good helpers like these and two capable
doctors to undertake a great part of the medical work, it
was now possible to organize the work. There were
always a certain number of Africans who, if supervised,
could help as orderlies and in other ways. The one thing
that held them up now was lack of space.

There were often as many as a hundred and twenty
patients in the hospital now, where formerly there had
been perhaps fifty, and there was no space in which to
expand and erect further buildings. It would have helped

to relieve the famine if only there had been some waste-
land near which could have been laid out as a plantation
and planted with crops. Then the hospital could have
been very largely self-supporting. The relatives who
accompanied each patient could have helped in the work
of laying out such a plantation, thought the doctor to
himself. Even the patients, when they were getting
better, might have given a little help.

Yes, if only there was more room! They *must* have
more room.

Day by day, when he had time to think, the Doctor
thought over this question and pondered it in his mind.
When October came he had reached a bold decision. He
would move the entire hospital to a new site farther up
the river, where there was more open space in which to
expand. All the time he had spent on rebuilding since
his return to Africa now seemed to him to be of no use.
But the corrugated iron which was coming from Europe
would now make roofs for a new hospital instead of the
old one.

It was characteristic of the Doctor to act like this. He
had always done so since he had first made up his mind
to become a doctor and be of use to his fellow-men. He
thought a thing out by himself, came to a decision, and
then let nothing turn him from it.

He did not say a word to anyone at first about this
decision to move the hospital, not even to the other
doctors and nurses. He went off alone by boat a mile
and three-quarters up-stream to a place he knew well,
where the river Ogowe divides into two branches. Once
upon a time there had been some African villages there,
so that the forest would not be so thick to clear as it
might be elsewhere, and also there were some useful
oil-palms.

He had to apply to the District Commissioner for permission to occupy this land, and the District Commissioner was very kind. He said that it would take some months to settle all the formalities to do with the acquisition of the land, but meantime Dr Schweitzer was given permission to start building.

When he got home again to his hospital he called the doctors and nurses together and told them of his plan. After their first astonishment, they broke into shouts of joy, which very much puzzled the African people who overheard them and wondered what the white people were so happy about.

Now that the hospital was to be moved plans had at once to be set in motion.

The first thing to do was to peg out the new area, and make a plan which could be shown to the District Commissioner. The doctors themselves supervised this job. Guided by a compass held in the hand, they cut tracks in the forest preparatory to taking measurements. While they were doing the pegging out and measuring, the actual clearance of the forest could be begun, and in this the Africans could help.

Every morning a procession set out from the hospital to take part in this work, the procession consisting of the friends of the patients and any patients who had been cured and were willing to help out of gratitude. Each helper was provided with an axe and bush-knife, which, to tell the truth they sometimes took rather unwillingly, for they did not like the idea of such hard work. Then every one climbed into the canoe, which took them the best part of two miles up-stream to the new site.

There was no payment for the workers, any more than there is regular payment for patients at the hospital, but every one who helped got a present and an extra-big ration of food. The presents they liked best were tobacco and spirits, but the Doctor would not give them these. He would only give useful things, such as spoons, cups, plates, knives, cooking-pots, blankets, mats, mosquito-nets, or material for clothes. So, urged on by the Doctor, they did succeed in doing some useful work each day. We have to remember that the Africans were rather like small children. They did not mind working their hardest for anything for which they could see a reason. For example, an African will row a canoe for hours to bring a friend to the hospital to be cured of some illness, or he will work for days at clearing ground to form a banana plantation. But it seemed as if they could not understand why all these trees were to be cut down and the ground levelled so that a new hospital might be built for others who would come after.

The Doctor's plan was to cut down the giant trees and, when they had been cut up, to stack the logs in piles so that they could make use of them later on for fuel. The enormous roots were to be left in the ground, and in between the roots and the stacks of logs crops would be sown. There were some oil-palms which were to be left standing, as they would come in very useful to furnish the oil which the Africans use for cooking. A few of the large trees were to be left standing too, to form shade when the new hospital was built.

Every night when work was over the procession had to be formed again, and back they all went in their canoes to the old hospital, where the doctor not in charge of the forestry party would have been working all day among the patients.

Darkness falls very suddenly at about six o'clock on the Equator, and sometimes a terrible thunderstorm breaks

quite suddenly at about that hour, so that the forestry
party had to keep a good look-out upon the weather so
as to return in time if a storm threatened.

Day after day this work of clearance went on, the
party setting out each morning and returning each
evening. When the year 1926 dawned things had pro-
gressed very well, and now the Doctor began to consider the actual building.

How different from European life was this life on the
edge of the primeval forest in Equatorial Africa! What
doctor in Europe would draw up plans for his own
hospital, undertake all the measurements, organize the
obtaining of the various materials for building, and then
with his own hands act as builder?

Dr Schweitzer had decided at once that these new
buildings were to take a more permanent form than those
at the old hospital. There were not to be any more
bamboo-huts or leaf-tile roofs. Of course, stone or brick
walls could not be considered; they would take far too
long to build and cost far too much money. So it was
decided that the walls should be of corrugated iron, and
that the whole should be built upon hundreds of hardwood piles into which the ants could not bore holes. All
the wards would be built like this, and they would
spread out along the river's edge. The hospital would
begin to look a little bit as it appears to-day.

The next thing was to obtain the piles. The Doctor
had learnt by experience at which places different things
were to be found, and he knew that there were some
hardwood trees of the sort needed about sixteen miles
up-stream. So to Dr Nessman, the 'little' doctor, was
entrusted the task of procuring the piles. He made his
first journey on January 4, 1926, and with the help of a
few Africans he brought back thirty. He had to go again

several times to bring back more, enough for the foundations to be started.

The piles had to have their ends charred to make them last longer, and after that had been done the job of driving the piles into the ground was begun. This, of course, was a most important thing, for the floors would be laid down on these piles, and there must be a strong foundation. At the bottom there must be a layer of stones, well stamped into the earth. Then the greatest care had to be taken that the tops of all the piles were exactly level, so that the beams to be placed on them would lie flat. The Africans could help in the planting of the piles (of which altogether there would be some hundreds), but for the getting of them into position Dr Schweitzer himself had to come to the rescue.

The first ward was to be about eighty feet long by sixteen feet wide. The floors were to be of wood, unlike the beaten-earth floors of the old hospital, and there was to be mosquito-proof netting. It was Dr Schweitzer's idea to build the wards long and narrow, so that the air could pass through to every patient. The wards were also to be built running east and west, so that the sun would never strike the side walls direct. These wards were later proved to be several degrees cooler than the older-fashioned square type of building.

At the end of February 1926, when the building had been going on for only a month or two, Dr Nessman had to return home to Europe to do his compulsory military service, but another doctor, Dr Trensz, was able to come out to Africa almost at once to take his place. He arrived before Dr Nessman had to leave, and so was able to be instructed how to obtain the piles from up the river, for now this would be one of his jobs.

By dint of much hard work on the part of all, superintended by the moving spirit Dr Schweitzer, who had done a great part of the work with his own hands, the piles needed for the whole hospital were at last fixed in place. Besides the large building, eighty feet by sixteen, there were to be four others, two larger still and the other two somewhat smaller. Then there was to be another ward higher up the river, especially for white patients, built upon forty-eight piles. The whole of it would really be almost like a little village when finished.

When the buildings themselves were to be begun on the foundations of piles there were three black African carpenters, but a white man was needed to supervise them. The Doctor sent to Europe to see if there was one who would come, and to his great joy Hans Muggensturm arrived from Switzerland on April 26, 1926, and at the same time came a new nurse, the sister of Dr Lauterburg (N'Tschinda N'Tschinda).

Now the building proceeded apace. Every ward would have to be roofed during the dry season before the middle of Spetember, and then, when the rains started, work at the inside fittings could be carried on.

There was also the Doctor's own house to be built on the hill above.

During the summer the Doctor's old assistant Joseph, who had come back to help him, decided to leave again. He was married now, and wanted to buy expensive European clothes for his wife instead of the ordinary clothing an African woman would wear. Joseph could get better wages from the timber-traders than the Doctor could afford him, and so, though he was very sorry to lose him, the Doctor could say nothing more about it. So they parted, but remained good friends, always willing to do one another a good turn when needed.

Dr Schweitzer on the site of the new leper village built with funds which he got with the Nobel Peace Prize award

By courtesy of Mrs Clara Urquhart

Dr Schweitzer inspects the foundations for the new leper village, which, when completed, will house three hundred patients

By courtesy of Mrs Clara Urquhart

It was at the beginning of 1927, just a year after the momentous decision to move the hospital had been made, that the new buildings were sufficiently complete for the patients to be taken there.

About the same time as the hospital was being moved an old man, miles away in Johannesburg, South Africa, was writing a book. Forty or fifty years ago he had been a trader in West Africa in the firm of Hatton and Cookson, and he had lived a very adventurous life among the Africans, many of whom were at that time cannibals. In his old age he was living in poor circumstances in Johannesburg when he attracted the notice of a lady novelist, Mrs Ethelreda Lewis, who, by inviting him to her house and getting him to talk, extracted from him an immense amount of thrilling information about West Africa as it was nearly half a century earlier. She encouraged him to write down his adventures and reminiscences, and they were later published as a book with the title *Trader Horn*.

The firm of Hatton and Cookson later moved to an island near by, and when Dr Schweitzer chose the new position for his hospital it was discovered that it was the very place where Hatton and Cookson's used to be and which Trader Horn would have known intimately as a young man. This interested the Doctor very much; he was so enterprising himself that he liked to think of this enterprising young man as having been there and knowing the places that he knew.

On January 21, 1927, the removal began from the old hospital to the new one up-stream, and some organization was needed.

Mlle Kottmann and Hans Muggensturm went on first to the new hospital to receive the patients, while Dr Lauterburg, Nurse Lauterburg, and Mlle Hausknecht

F

stayed behind at the old hospital to load the canoes with
whatever baggage had to be removed. Dr Schweitzer
himself spent the whole day on the river, towing full
canoes up-stream and bringing them back empty. Some
of the white patients lent their motorboats to assist.

By evening the last journey was made, and the last
of the patients settled into their new home. They were
delighted with it. From every side came cries: "This is
a good hut, Doctor—a good hut."

Things were beginning to look more as they would
look if you were to visit the Schweitzer hospital to-day,
though a very great deal has been added since then.
Still, it was a very long way away from the Doctor's
first fowlhouse hospital, with one nurse (his wife) and
one helper (Joseph) fourteen years ago. There was still
a lot of work to be done on the interiors of the wards,
but that could be gradually accomplished. The old
hospital, too, was to be demolished, and some of its
planks brought away to make more beds at the new
hospital. Dr Schweitzer and some of his helpers stayed
for a while longer at the old buildings to superintend
this, while the other two doctors and the other nurses
and helpers lived up at the new site.

Dr Trensz had soon to leave and return home, as he
only had permission to stay for a year, but already
another doctor and more helpers were arriving. The
Schweitzer hospital was becoming more and more
widely known, and more and more admirers of Dr
Schweitzer's work were anxious to give their help.

Two hundred and fifty patients and their attendants
could be received in the new buildings, and the hospital
began to look like a village, as we say. Besides the
buildings for the patients, the nurses, and the doctors,
a big shed had been built for the canoes and boats.

And now it was time that the Doctor himself should take a furlough. It was three years and a half since he had come out from Europe for his second sojourn in Africa. He began now to make arrangements to leave, and with him went two of his faithful helpers. But he could go with an easy heart this time, knowing that he had left his hospital in good hands.

It was in July 1927 that Dr Schweitzer left Africa for the second time. He knew that this was not the end of Africa for him, for he called it his "second home."

CHAPTER TEN

WAR AGAIN

DURING the next ten years Dr Schweitzer was to be away from his hospital for long periods at a time, but always, wherever he was and whatever he was doing, he carried his Africans in his heart.

In order to gain funds for his hospital he travelled round giving lectures in places as far apart as Sweden, Denmark, Holland, France, Switzerland, England, and Czechoslovakia. In between the visits he lived quietly with his wife and little daughter, Rhena, at Strasburg or at a holiday resort in the Black Forest.

In 1928, the year after his return from Africa, the city of Frankfurt presented him with a prize which was given every so often in memory of the great German poet Goethe. Goethe, besides being a poet, had, like Schweitzer, been much interested in the welfare of his fellow men. This "Goethe" prize was awarded for "Service to Humanity," and it was considered by the people of Frankfurt that Schweitzer well deserved it. He had to go to Frankfurt and make a long speech on Goethe, which was later translated into English.

With some of the money he received as the "Goethe" prize, he decided to build a little house in Günsbach, where he had lived as a child, and where his father had been pastor at the village church. The Doctor had begun his education at the village school with the village boys in Günsbach, and many of them were still alive—elderly men now, as he was. He remembered them all with affection, and, though he had risen to intellectual heights to which they had not been able to attain, this did not make him feel at all self-satisfied. He has told us that when he met his old school-fellows he still remembered which of them had been superior to him in various ways at the village school. One was better at mental arithmetic, one at geography, one never forgot a date, and one could write almost better than the schoolmaster himself.

So when he goes home to the little house at Günsbach all the people know and love him.

He built this little house not only for himself, but also so that any of his faithful hospital staff could use it as a home when they were on furlough. It is still used as such. When the district was bombed during the Second World War the little house remained undamaged.

After he had built it he felt as if he ought to do something more for other people, so he gave more lectures and more concerts and raised twenty thousand marks for German missions and German charities.

All the countries in which he played and lectured were now becoming interested in the hospital and anxious to help. Many of his friends in these countries gave large gifts to enable the hospital to grow. One lady sold her necklace and gave the money for a building which was called the Necklace building. Three London ladies gave another building—the River House.

A gentleman named Ambrose Pomeroy-Cragg, who had lived in London, had been moved during the First World War to do a very kindly deed. For a thousand nights, when London was in darkness during the black-out, he had been in the habit of meeting at Victoria Station the night trains carrying soldiers, whom he guided home. When he died subscriptions were raised in order to send a gift in his memory to the Lambaréné hospital, whose work he had greatly admired.

You will remember the rough wooden cell that Nöel Gillespie had put together for the poor mentally deranged patient. Now this money in memory of Mr Pomeroy-Cragg was to be used to build a ward so that the insane patients could be properly looked after. When it was built a plaque was put upon the wall with an inscription, which, translated into English, reads as follows:

In Europe, during the Great War, he guided the soldiers on leave through the darkness of London. To-day in Africa, in the depths of the primeval forest, at the Lambaréné hospital, in his name we receive and shelter those whose minds wander in darkness. Blest be his memory and may his spirit live ever in us.

Another gift was sent in memory of Dorothy Mannering. A well of pure water which never ran dry had been discovered at Lambaréné, and the Doctor and Mlle Emma Hausknecht with their own hands lined the well with 750 cement bricks to keep the walls from falling in. An inscription was cut into the cement: "In memory of Dorothy Mannering, this well of pure water so precious to all who benefit by it."

Still another gift, from St Botolph's Church, Bishopsgate, was a lamp to be placed at the landing-stage where patients so often arrived in the darkness of the tropical night.

While he was making friends and money by his organ-playing and lectures the words of his aunt at Mülhausen used to come back to him: "You never know what use your music may not be to you when you grow up." Certainly neither of them at that time foresaw that it would be used for helping to found a hospital for Africans on the edge of the primeval forest.

Among all his work he must have found some time to give his little girl music-lessons, for there is a picture of him doing this in 1930, when Rhena would have been eleven or twelve years old.

During these ten years he went back several times to Africa for short periods, and in 1937 he went back for the sixth time. He was now sixty-two years old. He stayed for two years and then went home again, arriving early in February 1939 at his little house in Günsbach.

And now the same sad thing was about to happen as had happened in August 1914—a quarter of a century before.

War!

What we now call the Second World War was in the air in Europe. Dr Schweitzer, newly arrived in Günsbach, decided that he ought to return to his hospital. He left the little house (eight years later visitors to his room found his calendar still at February 1939) and returned to Lambaréné by the same boat on which he had come. He knew that once war broke out communications between Europe and Africa would be cut, as they had been during the First World War. He ordered large stocks of medicines, and laid in large quantities of rice as soon as he arrived in Africa.

But there was no knowing how long the War would last, and at length, sad at heart, he had to decide that all the patients except those who were seriously ill must go home, as there was not food enough to feed them.

Just a few months before the War actually broke out one very pleasant thing happened. Rhena was now twenty years old and had been married to M. Eckert, an organ-builder, whom the family had known for several years. And now she and her mother came out to Lambaréné on a short visit. It was Rhena's first visit, and it gave her father much pleasure.

"I am so happy that my daughter is able to see the hospital," he wrote. "She is delighted with the six chimpanzees and the five young antelopes that play around in the yard."

They did not stay long, and before the War actually started she had rejoined her husband in Paris.

The next year, at the time of the collapse of the French Government, she, her husband, and their little baby had to escape. They travelled in their little car across France. "For about a month," Rhena wrote, "we lived on the roads, sleeping most of the time in our car, and eating when we found something to eat."

However, they eventually arrived safely at Lyons.

One good thing did come to the hospital indirectly through the War. There was more leisure, and more labourers were available, so that a great advance was made in the planting of fruit-trees in the orchard.

We need not linger long over this period. In 1940 the two forces of Vichy and of Free France fought over the little village of Lambaréné, their planes circling overhead. By mutual agreement both sides tried (and successfully) to spare the hospital. The Free French, under General de Gaulle, were the victors, and so French Equatorial Africa joined the Allies.

The Doctor's friends in Europe were fighting on the other side, which must have been a source of sadness to him. The whole idea of war and fighting was foreign to his nature, and he hated it.

The hospital work of necessity grew less. Some of the nurses left to find employment elsewhere, and four remained. Dr Schweitzer, helped by two competent doctors, stayed on to do what was possible among the patients who were still there. As time went on a very welcome helper appeared. It was the Doctor's wife, who had with difficulty managed to get a passage. She had been back again during the dry seasons occasionally since she had left in 1917 during the First World War, but she had not been able to stay in Africa during the wet seasons, when the climate is especially trying to a European.

Many white patients whose health was getting bad through too long a stay in the tropics, and who could not get a passage home, began to come for treatment to the Schweitzer hospital and were glad to be able to do so.

How anxiously people in England used to listen to the War news two or three times every day during the War years! But at Lambaréné there was no radio to call out: "This is the nine o'clock news." A bulletin came by telegraph twice a week to the village store, and from there it was spread to the mission and the hospital. That was all the news they got.

All the adults and some of the children in England to-day will remember May 8, 1945, the day we called VE (victory in Europe) Day, when at last the war in Europe came to an end. What excitement there was with us on that day!

When the news of peace reached the hospital at Lambaréné Dr Schweitzer, seventy years old, was sitting at his study table busy writing letters which had to be sent off that afternoon by the down-stream river-steamer. He did not rise, but went calmly on with his duty— these letters which must be ready when the river-steamer passed.

When they were finished he went down the hill from his house to the hospital, where some of his heart patients were waiting for him. Not until he had seen to

them did he have the bell rung and the news announced
that the war in Europe was at an end. Then, tired as he
was, the 'Old Doctor,' seventy years of age, went up the
hill past his house to the plantation to see if everything
was going on well there.

CHAPTER ELEVEN

VISITORS FROM AMERICA

SOON after the War had broken out Dr Schweitzer had written to some friends in America to say that he was not sure whether he would be able to keep the hospital open or whether he would be forced to close it and return to Europe. When he eventually decided to keep it open he wrote again to his friends to tell them.

The immediate result of this was that they set to work to found what was to be called the "Albert Schweitzer Fellowship of America" to maintain interest and to collect funds for him.

In 1946, when the War was over, the Secretary-Treasurer of this Fellowship with his wife travelled to Lambaréné to see the hospital and the Doctor for themselves. They wrote a little diary, from which the following is a short quotation:

We arrived after dark, about 7.30. In the blackness of the night our faithful African crew got us out of the launch. Across the sand we ploughed for what seemed a long way, up some rough stone steps, up and up, by our flashlights. Then into the black forest. But some lights began to flicker here and there, and suddenly we were outside windows. Inside we saw a long room, with a long table spread and folks round it. There were three or four kerosene lamps along the length of the table. Just as we glimpsed this scene, they heard us and began getting up from the table. By the time we got around to the door Dr Schweitzer was on the steps to greet us, and behind him Mrs Schweitzer. Thus it was that we met this man whom we have always considered great, but whose true greatness was to grow and impress

itself upon us in the few days we were privileged to spend
in his presence, and in the presence of the work which he
has hewn out of one of Africa's most jungled forests.

They go on to say:

The hospital is not exactly a New York Hospital. Dr
Schweitzer believes in keeping things, as much as possible,
on a level with the culture of the people. Yet with all its
crudeness it has a wonderful record both for quantity and
quality of work. Africans and Europeans alike swear by it
and flock to it for hundreds of miles around.[1]

The next year, 1947, two more American visitors,
Mr Charles Joy and Mr Melvin Arnold, who had long
been interested in what they had heard about Dr
Schweitzer and his hospital, decided to go and pay a
visit to it.

They set off by plane from Oregon, in the United
States, reaching the coast of Africa in about a day and a
half. The next part of the journey, by train, truck, and
canoe, took a week, and at the end of that time they stood
on the banks of the Ogowe river and shook hands with
Dr Schweitzer himself. They have written a wonderfully
interesting book called *The Africa of Albert Schweitzer*,[2]
illustrated with numbers of beautiful photographs, and
from this book we get a vivid description of the Doctor
himself and the hospital as it now is.

When the American visitors arrived at Lambaréné
it was thirty-four years since the Doctor's first arrival.
Then there was only one doctor (himself) one nurse and
housekeeper (his wife), one interpreter and hospital
orderly (Joseph), and a fowlhouse for a hospital. Now
there were forty different buildings—wards for black

[1] From a Postscript to *My Life and Thought*, written by Everett
Skillings, in the second edition, with a new chapter, 1954.
[2] Published by A. and C. Black (1949).

patients of various tribes, wards for white patients, wards for patients suffering from leprosy, cells for temporarily insane patients, store-rooms, houses for doctors, and houses for nurses.

Little babies, who in the old days would have been cast out to die because they had lost their mothers, were now cared for in the hospital.

Scores of acres of ground were under cultivation. There were peas, beans, tomatoes, and other crops in the garden, and an orchard full of fruit-trees. The Doctor believed very strongly in the goodness of fruit as food, and during the Second World War when the timber-trade was at a standstill and so he could get a good deal of help from the Africans, he grew thousands of little fruit-trees in a nursery and had them planted out. The result of this was that during the War he had so much fruit that he could exchange some of it for rice to feed the people. The European people who had their meals in the Doctor's house had fruit salad, made from pineapples, tangerines, and grape-fruit, every day for lunch and for dinner, and could have several helpings if they wished.

The African patients and their friends lived chiefly on bananas and manioc (a sort of tapioca in thick sticks). They were supposed to bring their own food when they came to the hospital, but if the Doctor found that any were too poor to do this he provided rations for them. The rations for each person were about six fairly large bananas and two sticks of manioc a day. They were given out at midday two or three times a week, and the people formed up in a queue, just as we do in England.

Each family or group had its own little fire and cooking-pot on three stones, and the bananas, after being skinned, were boiled and then dipped in palm-oil given out for the purpose. Out of the manioc sticks the people made a kind of bread. The sticks had first to be soaked for three or four days in running water to soak the poisons out of the roots. Then they were cut up, pounded into pulp, and kneaded into a kind of paste. This paste was wrapped in leaves and boiled, and the result was something like bread. When the meal was cooked each little group squatted round its own fire and ate and talked.

When the American visitors arrived they found all sorts of industries being carried on at the hospital. Large basketwork fish-traps were made, and reed mats, and a very strong kind of rope made from the fibres of pineapple-leaves. Some of the Africans can also make clothes—trousers, aprons, and overalls—using the sewing-machine, and mattresses are made and stuffed with kapok. The kapok-trees are growing near, and the stuff we call kapok is the fluff which surrounds the nuts.

There is a laundry on the premises, and a tinsmith's shop and a miniature smithy for mending broken tools. All these things had gradually taken shape during the years. There was an old African shoemaker, called Basile A'Atombogogno, who had been at the hospital since its very early days and was still working there.

The American visitors have described the way in which the days at the hospital were usually spent.

At 6.30 each morning all the workmen assemble, and the Doctor comes out and assigns to them their various duties. Perhaps some will be told to weed the garden, or to dig, or transplant. On the particular day which is described water had to be fetched from the river, for the pump had broken down, and the Doctor himself had to set to and mend it.

At midday all return from their various employments

for lunch. The African people cook and eat theirs in their own way. The American visitors will join Dr Schweitzer and the other Europeans in the dining-hall. The Doctor says grace very softly in French, and then the meal begins. It is a very cheery meal. At one o'clock after lunch comes an hour's siesta or rest. In most hot countries people take a siesta during the hottest part of the day. "Without it we could not work," says the Doctor, but the American visitors notice that on the particular day they are describing the Doctor himself takes no siesta.

The siesta over, there is another roll-call at two o'clock, and then every one is set to work again.

The day wears on. Night comes swiftly in the tropics, and soon after six darkness falls. This is the time when the Doctor likes to have a short time for relaxation. Now he has time to talk a little to his visitors and to pet his antelopes. However, one must not linger long, for the poisonous mosquitoes will soon be coming out.

Then comes dinner, and after dinner the Doctor goes to the piano and plays a hymn to be sung. He says quietly in French some verse from the Bible, and every one says the Lord's Prayer together. After a little while, on this particular evening, the Doctor comes over to one of his visitors and asks: "Would you like to come and see my quarters?" The visitor is glad to go, and, taking lanterns in case of snakes, they go along the path which leads from the dining-room to the Doctor's house. They step in, shutting the door quickly behind them, for the mosquitoes will be about. Now they enter the Doctor's little study-bedroom. Here is his bed, with mosquito-net, and the table at which he works, and the little wooden seat with no back on which he sits when working. "I worked on this seat without a cushion till I was

seventy," he tells his visitors. Now he allows himself a
little cushion. In this room too he stores tools, and
paddles and pails, one within the other, and all the
various things which he will have to give out to his black
workmen to-morrow, but which he must keep in his
own room for safety.

. After a little while they go into the adjoining room.
Here is the famous piano with the organ-pedals which
was given to Dr Schweitzer by the Bach Society of
Paris when he first came to Lambaréné in 1913 so that
he need not be quite cut off from his beloved music. It
sounds strange but very beautiful to the American
visitor to hear Bach's music played out here in Africa
in the loneliness of the great primeval forest. In a corner
of this room is a little wire enclosure for the baby antelopes. During the day they run loose, and the Doctor
spreads a rug over the organ-pedals lest a little fawn
should break its leg among them. At night they sleep in
their little wire-pen, and the bigger antelopes sleep
outside under the house, which is raised from the ground.

At half-past eight a gong sounds outside. It is a cur-
few, and all the little fires must be put out now and the
black people go to bed. The Doctor takes his visitor
back to his little study-bedroom. He pulls down from
the shelves above him piles of written sheets of paper and
shows them to the visitor. These are the pages of the
book he is writing—*The Philosophy of Civilization*. As
each chapter is finished he piles it on the shelves, and
the unfinished chapters are hung by strings to nails.
He tries to do a little writing each evening, but if there
are any seriously ill patients at the hospital he gives his
attention to them instead. His correspondence is very
large, and sometimes there are sacks full of letters
awaiting answers.

Dr Schweitzer lends a hand to show how it should be done.
Much of the actual physical labour of building the new
leper village has been done by the octogenarian doctor
By courtesy of Mrs Clara Urquhart

Dr Schweitzer with one of his cured lepers who has remained to work at the hospital. It will be seen how his muscles have developed as a result of the manual work on the new leper village

By courtesy of Mrs Clara Urquhart

The time passes, and at last the Doctor rises and says good-night. The visitor departs, shutting the door quickly on account of the mosquitoes. He remains standing for a little while outside the house, breathing in the fresh air. After a few minutes he sees the door open again, and the Doctor comes out, wearing his old felt hat. It is one o'clock in the morning. Seeing the visitor standing there, the Doctor tells him he is just going down to the hospital to pay a last visit to his patients before going to bed, as he usually does. He invites the visitor to go with him, and they set off down the hill together. Some of the black patients are asleep, some are still awake. They like the Doctor to come round and say good-night. He passes from cot to cot, saying a kind word here and there. When the round is over he climbs the hill again and goes to his own room. The visitor goes to his room, and reads a little, late though it is. When at length he settles down to sleep he sees by the light in the Doctor's room that the Doctor is still working.

The American visitors have described what took place on Midsummer Day, June 24, at the Schweitzer Hospital during their visit. This is St John the Baptist's Day, and in Alsace, where Dr Schweitzer's home is, it is the custom to light large bonfires. So the Doctor had decided that there should be a bonfire here too on the banks of the Ogowe river.

After dinner, instead of separating and going to their own rooms, everybody joined to form a procession down to the riverside, carrying lanterns in their hands. The bonfire was lighted and boughs of trees thrown upon it till the flames mounted higher and higher, and the dancing figures could be seen dark against their bright light, and the background of the river.

When next Sunday came the Doctor gave a simple

G

little sermon on St John the Baptist to his African people. A little service was always held on Sundays in between the wards, and every one who was able to come had to be there. Many of the Africans who came were heathens and had probably never heard a Christian sermon before. The Doctor gives his sermon in French, and on either side of him stands an African to act as interpreter. One of them translates each sentence into the Galoa language, and the other into the Pahouin language, for most of the Africans know one or the other of these languages.

When the Doctor gives the sermon he preaches about simple things that the Africans will understand. He often takes one of the parables as a subject, such as the Prodigal Son or the Good Samaritan. There is singing too at the service. Nobody has a hymn-book, but some of the Africans know by heart hymns that they have learnt at the mission, and they will sing them lustily and with enjoyment.

The days passed on, and at last the visit of the Americans to Lambaréné was at an end and they had to return home to the United States. With them went the photographs they had taken, the notes they had made, and the memory of all they had seen and heard at the Schweitzer hospital. Out of all this they shaped their book *The Africa of Albert Schweitzer* as a tribute of admiration to the doctor himself.

It might be of interest to read the whole of one sermon which Dr Schweitzer gave to his Africans upon the subject of forgiveness. Of course, the Africans who went to the mission school received instruction in the Bible there and regularly attended the mission services, but down at the hospital, where they come and go quickly, one cannot give any connected teaching, and so the Doctor tried to give them something which they could carry away in their hearts and perhaps understand later, rather in the way in which our Lord used to deliver His parables to the crowds.

The Bible records how St Peter had asked whether he ought to forgive his brother as often as seven times, and our Lord had replied, "I say not unto thee Until seven times: but Until seventy times seven." Here, then, is the sermon, which was given in French and translated by the interpreter into the Galoa and Pahouin tongues.

Scarcely are you up in the morning and standing in front of your hut when somebody whom all know to be a bad man comes and insults you. Because the Lord Jesus says that one ought to forgive, you keep silent instead of beginning a palaver.

Later on your neighbour's goat eats the bananas you were relying on for your dinner. Instead of starting a quarrel with the neighbour, you merely tell him it was his goat, and that it would be the right thing if he would make it up to you in bananas. But when he contradicts you and maintains that the goat was not his, you quietly go off and reflect that God has made so many bananas to grow in your plantation that there is no need for you to begin a quarrel on this account.

A little later comes the man to whom you gave ten bunches of bananas in order that he might sell them for you at the market along with his own. He brings the money for only nine. You say, "That's too little." But he retorts, "You made a mistake in counting, and only gave me nine bunches." You are about to shout in his face that he is a liar. But then you can't help thinking about many lies, of which you alone know, for which God must forgive you, and you go quietly into your hut.

When you want to light your fire you discover that somebody has carried off the wood that you fetched out of the forest yesterday, intending it to serve you for a week's cooking. Yet again you compel your heart to forgive, and refrain from making a search round all your neighbours' huts to see who can possibly have taken your wood so that you may bring an accusation against the thief before the headman.

In the afternoon when you are about to go and work in your plantation, you discover that some one has taken away your good bush-knife and left you in its place his old one, which has a jagged edge. You know who it is, for you recognize the bush knife. But then you consider that you have forgiven four times and that you may want to forgive even a fifth time. Although it is a day on which you have experienced much unpleasantness, you feel as jolly as if it had been one of your happiest. Why? Because your heart is happy in having obeyed the will of the Lord Jesus.

In the evening you want to go out fishing. You put out your hand to take the torch which ought to be standing in the corner of your hut. But it isn't there. Then you are overcome by anger, and you think that you have forgiven enough for to-day, and that now you will lie in wait for the man who has gone fishing with your torch. But yet once more the Lord Jesus becomes master of your heart. You go down to the shore with a torch borrowed from a neighbour.

There you discover that your boat is missing. Another man has gone fishing in it. Angrily you hide behind a tree in order to wait for him who has done you this wrong, and when he comes back you mean to take all his fish away from him and accuse him before the District Officer, so that he will have to pay you just compensation. But while you are waiting, your heart begins to speak. It keeps on repeating the saying of Jesus that God cannot forgive us our sins if we do not forgive each other. You have to wait so long that the Lord Jesus yet again gains the mastery over you. Instead of going for the other fellow with your fists, when at last in the grey of the morning he returns and tumbles down in a fright as you step out from behind the tree you tell him that the Lord Jesus compels you to forgive him and you let him go in peace. You don't even ask him to give up the fish when he does not leave them to you of his own accord. But I believe he does give them to you from sheer amazement that you don't start a quarrel with him.

Now you go home, happy and proud that you have succeeded in making yourself forgive seven times. But if the Lord Jesus were to come into your village on that day, and you were to step in front of Him and think He would praise you for it before all the people, then he would say to you, as to Peter, that seven times is not enough, but that you must forgive yet seven times and yet again and yet again, and yet many more times before God can forgive you your sins. . . ."[1]

[1] From *Albert Schweitzer*, by G. Seaver, published by A. and C. Black (1951).

CHAPTER TWELVE

THE 'OLD DOCTOR'

THE following year, 1948, after nearly ten years in Africa without a furlough, Dr Schweitzer came home again to Europe, to the little house he had built with the money from the "Goethe" prize.

He was seventy-three years old now, and it was thirty-six years since he had first set out with his wife to Africa to found his hospital in the forest. He was very tired indeed, but a visit to the Black Forest and then to Switzerland put new life into him. In Switzerland he had the great joy of seeing his daughter Rhena and her husband, and (for the first time) his grandchildren, of whom there were now four. Although he had never before seen the children he had had them in his mind. A book had been published called *An Anthology of Albert Schweitzer*, containing extracts taken from all the books he had written. The publishers offered to send some copies to any of Schweitzer's friends and well-wishers whom he cared to name. He wrote back and said: "I want the first four copies to go to the grand-children whom I have never seen."

And so the years go on, and the 'Old Doctor,' as he is called in Africa, still goes on too. He was back again in England in 1952, and played for a few of his friends on the organ of St Margaret's Church, Westminster.

He is a modest man and cares little for recognition or praise for himself but much for his hospital. However, in spite of this, several world-renowned honours have lately been awarded to the 'Old Doctor.'

In 1952 he received the Swedish Nobel Peace prize for that year. He was also installed as a member of the French Academy.

In 1953 he was given the "Wellcome" medal of the Royal African Society for "dedicated service to Africa." There was a money award given with this medal, and Dr Schweitzer characteristically used it not for his own needs in his old age but on behalf of his hospital, for a special work.

This new addition was a village which is being built especially for patients—men, women, and children—suffering from the terrible disease of leprosy.

From the very first days of the hospital Africans suffering from leprosy used to come to it. They knew that the white doctor could not really cure them, for in those days people knew much less about the disease than they do now and it was not possible to cure it completely. But a man suffering from leprosy was often very unkindly treated in his own village, and indeed he was usually turned out of it, and so the lepers used to find their way to the Schweitzer Hospital, knowing that at any rate they would be kindly dealt with and well looked after.

However, as years went on new medicines were discovered, and within the last ten years or so some called sulphones have been found which, if continued with for a long enough period, can practically cure leprosy. In fact, if the treatment is started in an early enough stage of the disease and continued for a period of from two to five years it is possible to effect a complete cure.

The problem was: "Where should lepers undergoing this treatment live for so long a time?" In 1950 there were fifty or sixty of them, in 1951 there were a hundred, in 1952 two hundred and in 1953 nearly three hundred. In 1954 there might well be four hundred and in 1955 perhaps still more, for they come in as they hear of the white doctor's wonderful drugs.

Up to 1953 they had lived in little bamboo-huts roofed with leaves which they built themselves around the large building of hardwood and corrugated iron. Then Dr Schweitzer, thinking the matter over, came to a decision, as he had come to other decisions in the earlier days of the hospital's history. His decision was to build a special village, seven minutes' walk away from the main buildings, for the lepers to live in while they were being cured.

It must have needed a good deal of planning, but when the planning was done it had been decided to have a large building for treatments, a smaller one for operations, then dressing-rooms and a laboratory, and finally the rooms in which the patients would live. There were to be eight or nine separate houses, each containing a number of small rooms, some more and some less, and in each little room two or three patients would live. The floors were to be of concrete, the walls of hardwood, and the roofs of corrugated iron. There was to be a veranda along the front of each house, and a tiny kitchen at the back of each little room, where the patients would prepare and cook their own meals.

It might seem rather luxurious and extravagant to have a separate kitchen for each room, but there is a reason for this. Africans unused to European ways will not eat anything that has not been cooked by themselves or their relatives. They are suspicious of food prepared by strangers, and, as they might have to spend several years living like this, away from their own villages, Dr Schweitzer wished it to be as "home-like" as possible. This was a very wise, as well as kind, idea of his, for otherwise a patient might get homesick and return to his village before the cure was complete.

The 'Old Doctor,' as he is affectionately called, is superintending and helping to build this village himself, as he built the hospital in bygone days. He has, as his second-in-command, the old black carpenter Monenzalie, who also helped him in the past, and has been connected with the hospital for over thirty years. Other help comes from some of the patients themselves, and the building of the village proceeds apace. Dr Schweitzer was seventy-eight years old when he began the work, and it was to this that he gave the money which he had received as the "Wellcome" prize.

To read about the growth of the hospital is more interesting than to read about the 'balance sheet,' but we must just say a word or two about this.

When Dr Schweitzer first went out to Lambaréné he took with him enough money to run the hospital for two years. He was quite prepared for his experiment to be a failure. He has told us this himself. But instead it was a success, and as he stayed more than two years he found himself in debt to the French mission under which he was working, and before he could pay off this debt, the First World War had broken out and he was sent as a prisoner to Europe. Later, as we have seen, the debts were able to be paid off.

But when we examine the balance sheet for 1952 we find that instead of debt there was a balance in hand of nine thousand pounds. That sounds good, but in the following year it was even better and the balance was more than eleven thousand pounds. This money comes from all over Europe, and also from places as far off as America and even New Zealand. What does Dr Schweitzer do with it all, for we may be sure he spends very little on

himself? The greater part of it, of course, goes to
Lambaréné to help pay the bills for feeding and doctoring the immense number of patients who now come to
the hospital every year.

From the money that remains Dr Schweitzer keeps
back some to form a fund at home in Europe. He
realizes that the time must come when those who have
helped him for so many years will have to give up their
work in Africa. This fund is being formed to give them
a little pension to live on.

Every few months Dr Schweitzer himself, or one of
his helpers, writes a little Bulletin which is printed and
sent round to people who are interested in the hospital.
Every time there is something new to report, some fresh
addition to the hospital which began over forty years
ago in a fowlhouse and now comprises more than forty
separate buildings. The latest addition, the Leper
Village, is the one to which the Doctor gave the money
which he had received from the Royal African Society.

An old friend of Dr Schweitzer, Jacques Feschotte,[1]
has lately written a book about him, and he describes
something of what he has seen when staying at the little
house in Günsbach.

Schweitzer's little room for working in is very simply
furnished. His jacket and his big black hat hang like two
dark shadows on the white-painted door. The room
looks right on to the street where he can see and greet
those who pass by. As the village people walk past they
often lay little offerings on the windowsill, as tokens of
love and respect—a few grapes, apples or radishes.

Jacques Feschotte has told us how Schweitzer loves

[1] *Albert Schweitzer: An Introduction*, published by A. and C.
Black (1954).

to go in the evenings up the quiet road to the little church to play the organ for a while, the organ he himself had restored in 1928. He and his brother and sisters had walked this road as children, and he remembers with gratitude how their parents had trained them to keep Sunday quietly and well, and wonders if the children now growing up will teach their children the same.

While the two friends sit together Schweitzer's thoughts wander out to Africa. "It'll be quiet at Lambaréné too," he says.

Dr Joy, one of the Americans who visited him at Lambaréné in 1947, has also written about Schweitzer and the little village church of Günsbach, and its organ.

"The little church must be full of memories for him," he writes.

"There in the high pulpit his father had preached. There on the other side from the pulpit his mother had had her place among the women. He and his brother and sisters had sat with the other children in the front pews, where he could see through the chancel screen the angels of the Catholic altar, for the church has always been used for both Protestant and Catholic services. Up where he now sits he had begun as a small boy of nine to play the organ. And now he is there again alone with his music and his memories, his heart singing forth its pæans of praise and prayer in the little village church as in a great cathedral."

New ways of life have become general since he was young—among them the wireless and the gramophone. Perhaps some day you may see in the window of a music shop a gramophone-record of a Bach Prelude and Fugue or some other piece recorded by Albert Schweitzer on Günsbach church organ. People will say: "Günsbach Church? Where is Günsbach? I've never heard of it"; for it is only a little village among the Vosges mountains.

But you who have read this book will know and will be able to say: "Günsbach is the little village where Dr Albert Schweitzer was brought up and spent his childhood, and he himself has restored the organ and made these records on it. And he has a little house in Günsbach which he built out of money given him by the people of Frankfurt as a prize for "Service to Humanity" in memory of Goethe."

In the same music-shop you may perhaps see a fat book, entitled *Bach—Musician-poet*, by Albert Schweitzer, translated by Dr Ernest Newman. This will be the English translation of Schweitzer's big German book on Bach which he wrote years ago, after having already written a French one.

Or you may see two or more volumes of *Organ Works by J. S. Bach*, edited by C. M. Widor and A. Schweitzer, and you will know that these were the works he and Widor began to edit together when he was Widor's organ pupil in Paris, long before he became a doctor. Widor himself wrote a preface to these volumes in which he has paid a tribute to his pupil Schweitzer.

As Schweitzer knew very well the old Lutheran texts, I explained to him my uncertainty in the presence of certain works of Bach, my inability to comprehend certain chorales which passed abruptly from one order of ideas to another, from the chromatic to the diatonic scale, from slow movements to rapid ones without apparent logical reason. What can the composer's thought be, what did he want to say? If he breaks the thread of his discourse in this way he must have another purpose than that of pure music, he must want to emphasize some literary idea. . . . but how are we to know this idea? "Simply by the words of the hymn," replied Schweitzer, and then he recited the words of the Chorale in question, which completely justified the musician and showed the flexibility of his descriptive powers when

dealing with the text word by word; it had been impossible
to appreciate the composition without understanding the
significance of the assumed words.[1]

So Widor had come to the conclusion that an edition
of the Chorale Preludes of Bach ought to be published
with the words of the old Lutheran hymns printed above
to help other organists to understand what Bach's
purpose had been, and he also realized that the best
person to undertake this was Schweitzer himself, who
knew both the music and the words. It is a surprise to a
great many people to know that the man who has
written these great books, and edited these great works,
and made these gramophone-records, and restored these
organs (yes, and written a book upon the restoration and
building of organs), and given these lectures and these
concerts, has also given his life to the founding of the
Schweitzer Hospital at Lambaréné on the Ogowe river,
and that he was still at the age of eighty taking an active
part in the running of the hospital.

Now our story is almost told, and there is nothing
more to relate about the hospital until the next little
Bulletin arrives from Lambaréné to tell us the latest news
of the progress of the leper village.

One thing, however, must not pass without notice,
and that is the speech which Dr Schweitzer delivered at
Oslo on November 4, 1954, in connexion with the Nobel
Peace prize which he had been awarded two years before.
In this speech he begs that the nations of the world may
all work together for peace. This cannot be done, he
says, merely by nationalism. We must all work for peace
by showing love not only to the people of our own nation,
but to people of other nations, and to all living creatures.
As St Paul has said: "If it be possible, as much as lieth

[1] From *Music in the Life of Albert Schweitzer.*

in you, live peaceably with all men." (Romans xii, 18.)

On January 14, 1956, Dr Albert Schweitzer celebrated his eighty-first birthday; more than half his long life has been spent in serving the African people. In October 1955 he paid one of his short periodical visits to England, where another honour was bestowed upon him. On October 19, he went to Buckingham Palace to be invested by the Queen with the Order of Merit, awarded to a very few people for conspicuous service. And so, when you have finished reading this story of the way in which the hospital has grown and spread, and goes on growing and spreading, you can picture it a little and feel that you know something about him—this man, who, at the age of twenty-one, made the decision from which he never looked back, that in gratitude for his own good health and happy childhood he would give himself to help others who were not so fortunate.